About This Author

I WAS BORN IN A THUNDER BURST OF COSMIC DUST IN THE ONENESS OF ALL THAT BE, MANIFESTING IN THE ILLUSIONARY UNIVERSITY OF LIGHT IN ALL ITS DENSITIES AND VIBRATORY FORMS, FOR I THE ETERNAL SINGULAR CELL OF THE WHOLE COSMIC CONSCIOUSNESS COLLECTIVE, BEING CONNECTED TO ALL THAT BE IN THE CREATION, THE BRAHMAN, THE WHOLE, FOR WE ARE ALL ONE in the oneness of all that be in the sea of cosmic light, a swirling of energy, electromagnetism, the weak and strong nuclear forces and gravity, DIVINE ETERNAL IMMORTAL INTER- DIMENSIONAL ANGELIC LIGHT BEINGS OF ULTRA VIOLET ENERGETIC CONSCIOUSNESS, CREATING AN AVATAR A BIOLOGICAL HUMAN FORM BODY FOR EXPERIENCE,

TO PAY KARMA, AND
MANIFESTING IN FROM THE
ETERNAL TO RAISE HUMANITIES
COLLECTIVE CONSCIOUSNESS,
FOR SPIRIT I BE FOR ENERGY I
SEE, ALL AROUND ME MULTI-
DIMENSIONALLY THIS IS JUST
HOW IT BE YOU SEE, FREQUENCY
VIBRATING LIGHT IN WAVE AND
POWDERED FORM TO, OPENING
PORTHOLES OUTSIDE TIME AND
SPACE FROM WHERE WE COME,
HOME IT BE IN THE ETERNAL
REALM OF THE KINGDOM OF
LIGHT, allowing humans that have
ascended opened their eternal light
bodies and stopped the cycles of life
and death, to evolve to HomoSapien,
HomoLuminous, we call upon
illuminated beings, on buddha beings,
and our ancestors at this time for
transformation to evolve to
metamorphosis in the rainbow angelic
light beings we be in our true nature,
we open our light bodies via our DNA
within are the schematics of the blue

THE COLLAPSE OF THE WORLD ILLEGAL STATUE LAW, SO THE COLLAPSE OF THE ILLEGAL BIRTH CERTIFICATE FRAUD & MONETARY SYSTEM, THE MANIFESTATION OF A NEW GLOBAL QUANTUM SYSTEM OF TRUTH CREATING THE INFINITY OF TRUTH SYSTEM, FOR COMMON LAW OF THE LAND, A NEW MONETARY SYSTEM BASED ON GOLD STANDARD NOT ETERNAL EMBODIED HUMAN AVATARS AS COLLATERAL, THE UNITED STATES CITIZEN THAT SAVED AMERICA & THE WORLD FROM ONE OF THE AGENDAS OF THE DISGRACED ROYAL FALLEN BLOODLINES OF LUCIFERS GENOCIDE & BECAME THE NEW WORLDS POST MASTER
BY
LOVELIFELEE

PAGE INDEX AT BACK OF BOOK

Published in 2020 by FeedARead.com Publishing

Copyright © The author as named on the book cover.

The author or authors assert their moral right under the Copyright, Designs and Patents Act, 1988, to be identified as the author or authors of this work.

All Rights reserved. No part of this publication may be reproduced, copied, stored in a retrieval system, or transmitted, in any form or by any means, without the prior written consent of the copyright holder, nor be otherwise circulated in any form of binding or cover other than that in which it is published and without a similar condition being imposed on the subsequent purchaser.

A CIP catalogue record for this title is available from the British Library.

print of your light body and access it will and quantum leap ten thousand years into our becoming, allowing us to be fully embodied on this 4th/5th dimensional earth planet and at the same time we can travel the stars at instant will teleporting to and fro and accessing the eternal kingdom of light realms, blessed i be for magic i see all around me in powdered light illusionary form divine spirit it be gravity, i see eternal transcendental oneness of all that be in creation you see blessings namaste lovelifelee.

OTHER BOOKS BY LOVELIFELEE

**THE SCAFFOLDING OF LIFE
THE WONDERFUL WORLD OF
GEOMETRIC MATTER
THE BUILDING BLOCKS
OF ALL BIOLOGICAL LIFE &
OUR UNIVERSE
ACCESS THE BLUE PRINT IN
YOUR DNA
GROW A RAINBOW LIGHT BODY
STOP KARMIC CYCLES & EVOLVE
TRANSCEND TIME & SPACE
ASCENSION YOU WILL ACHIEVE
BY LOVE LIFE LEE**

THE SCAFFOLDING OF LIFE
THE BUILDING BLOCKS OF SACRED GEOMETRY
LEARN THE SECRETS OF OUR PHYSICAL UNIVERSE
AND BIOLOGICAL MAKE UP OF OUR DNA, HOW TO
EVOLVE CONSCIOUSLY TRANSCEND TIME & SPACE
TO LEARN HOW TO TRANSVERSE THE
UNIVERSE WITH THOUGHT MIND BODY & SPIRIT
USING YOUR CONSCIOUS ENERGY
USING YOUR LIFE FORCE
UNDERSTAND YOUR FULL POTENTIAL GROW
A NEW BODY INTO BEING CONSCIOUSLY EVOLVE
AND ASCEND CREATE A RAINBOW BODY OF
LIGHT YOUR DIVINE RIGHT

FRONT COVER

WISDOM OF MAGICAL WONDER
WISDOM MAGICAL IN NATURE
WISDOM OF SPLENDOUR
FROM THE MINDS EYE & HEART SPACE

OF LOVE LIFE LEE

THROUGH THIS BOOK MESSAGES OF ANCIENT
KNOWLEDGE AND WISDOM ABOUT ACCESSING
YOUR FULLEST POTENTIAL AS A HUMAN BEING
LEARNING TO ACCESS YOUR DNA THROUGH
DISCIPLINE'S PRACTICE'S MEDITATION YOGA
SHAMANIC CEREMONIES PLANT MEDICINES
AYAHUASCA CEREMONIES ASTAL TRAVEL
DREAMS SPIRIT WORLD DIET PART OF THE KEY
AND EVOLVE CONSCIOUSLY GROW A BODY OF LIGHT
FROM THE BLUE PRINT IN YOUR DNA
TRANSCEND TIME AND SPACE
TRANSVERSE THE UNIVERSE TRAVEL THE
HYPER-DIMENSIONAL MATRIX IN YOUR RAINBOW
BODY OF LIGHT
YOU ARE AN IMMORTAL INTERDIMENSIONAL LIGHT
BEING OF ULTRA VIOLET CONSCIOUSNESS ENERGY
ANGELIC DIVINE INFINITE YOU BE
IN AN OCEAN OF LIGHT IN THE ONENESS OF THE
WHOLE CREATION

Spiritual knowledge of the journey
Within and without gaining the understanding
of the scaffolding of life the building blocks of the magical
world of geometric matter the dodecahedrons & tetrahedrons
and life force energy of our selfs and our universe understand
frequencies light vibration in sacred geometry it's wisdom
connecting to the stars
Connecting to nature
Connecting to Energy fields
An awakening , the shaman and i am
A spirit being
An Immortal Interdimensional Light Being
OF Conscious Energy
Divine we be you and me by Divine Decree
Namaste
Blessings to all that be in the oneness of all the creation

BACK PAGE

THE SCAFFOLDING OF LIFE

THE SCAFFOLDING OF LIFE THE WONDERFUL WORLD OF GEOMETRIC MATTER THE BUILDING BLOCKS OF ALL BIOLOGICAL LIFE & OUR UNIVERSE ACCESS THE BLUE PRINT IN YOUR DNA GROW A RAINBOW LIGHT BODY STOP KARMIC CYCLES & EVOLVE TRANSCEND TIME & SPACE ASCENSION YOU WILL ACHIEVE

The scaffolding of life the wonderful world of geometric matter this book gives information on how to access and open your eternal immortal light body, On the building blocks of matter how your avatar your body is built and that of the reality around you it explains how the scaffolding of life is built through the building blocks of geometry, and the energies behind it the driving forces, behind the nucleus, electrons and black holes, the forces of electromagnetism, gravity, the weak and strong nuclear forces.

It explains how to stop the cycles of life and death to open your eternal light body, via diet, disciplines, and supplements and via monatomic elements the eight colloidal metals we have at birth in our bodies and never get again through food or water.

It explains the sacred geometric matter shapes of how the cells are built by dodecahedrons and their relationship to amino acids and of the tetrahedrons in side the dodecahedrons that relate to the proteins from our intake of food our diet. Also discussed are power planets and their access to the universe, other dimensions of reality in the hyper-dimensional matrix of creation.

The language of the building blocks of life are discussed, our luminous energy fields around are bodies that is the software that informs the hardware the DNA to grow the avatar the body. The torus fields are discussed, also the illusion of light in our universe the university for souls to experience and grow spiritually, the mandelbhrot fractal the building structure of our physical universe is explained via a complex mathematical numbers, also the five geometric shapes are looked at and their relationship to sound, vibrational frequencies.

The chakras the keys to the life force systems and to access travel in the energetic holographical universe are touched on, the energy wave of ascension is looked at, along with DNA upgrade, the law of one, breath control, diet, plant medicines, religious dogma and the shamanic Munay-Ki rites of initiation are discussed, and ascension, our bodies and the universe is a puzzle to be solved, to evolve and transverse.

OTHERS BOOKS BY LOVELIFELEE

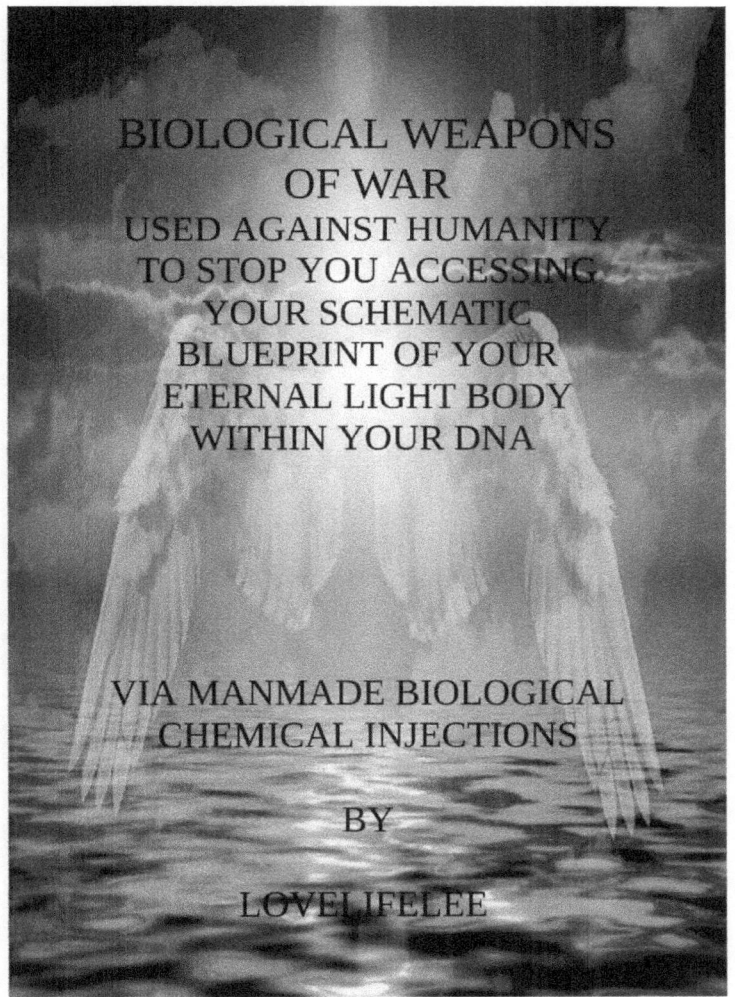

FRONT COVER

This short book explains the truth behind the psychological warfare conducted on the public & biological weapon vaccines, the intention behind them from the fallen angels cult to not only to cull a large portion of humanity in their eugenics program, but from the highest levels of understanding, from the spiritual god conscious perspective, from the awakened human being to that of their eternal immortality, on the understanding that the vaccines will stop you accessing your light body, via a schematic blueprint in your DNA, also this book explains our cells and their function and relationship to poisons.
This book also has an introduction to the DNA blue print of instructions to grow a light body.

BACK COVER

BIOLOGICAL WEAPONS OF WAR USED AGAINST HUMANITY TO STOP YOU ACCESSING YOUR DNA

This book has the truth of vaccines, the people behind the vaccines and their agendas, they are members of the two fallen angel royal Israelite Davidic bloodlines, a cult of blood sacrifice, the truth that the vaccines are not just to cull and mass murder 90% of humanity, but to put nano technologies in your body to delete your ancestral information and rewrite your DNA, then you are not the original DNA strain of human on earth, the fallen angel bloodlines corporations then can patent and own you.

Their main agenda is to stop you and humanities future children from accessing your schematic blueprint in your DNA, that allows you to open and access your eternal light body, allowing you to stop the cycles of life and death, and allowing you to ascend.

This means you can be fully embodied living on a 4th/5th dimensional earth but able to travel in the stars, the cosmos in the hyper- dimensional matrix at will via instant teleportation, and by opening a sixty foot field of light around your body and travelling through the sun filaments from solar system to solar system.

Vaccines are biological weapons of war against you and your children against humanity, against eternal immortal light being angels manifesting in to earth to have a human experience.

The elite royal fallen angel cult are evil, they are a death cult of mass murder, genocide to all cultures and faiths on earth, for they are an invading extraterrestrial parasite race of blood sacrifice.

This short book explains the truth behind the psychological warfare conducted on the public & biological weapon vaccines, the intention behind them from the fallen angels cult to not only to cull a large portion of humanity in their eugenics program, but from the highest levels of understanding, from the spiritual god conscious perspective, from the awakened human being to that of their eternal immortality, on the understanding that the vaccines will stop you accessing your light body, via a schematic blueprint in your DNA, also this book explains our cells and their function and relationship to poisons.

This book also has an introduction to the DNA blue print of instructions to grow a light body.

OTHER BOOKS BY LOVELIFELEE

FRONT COVER

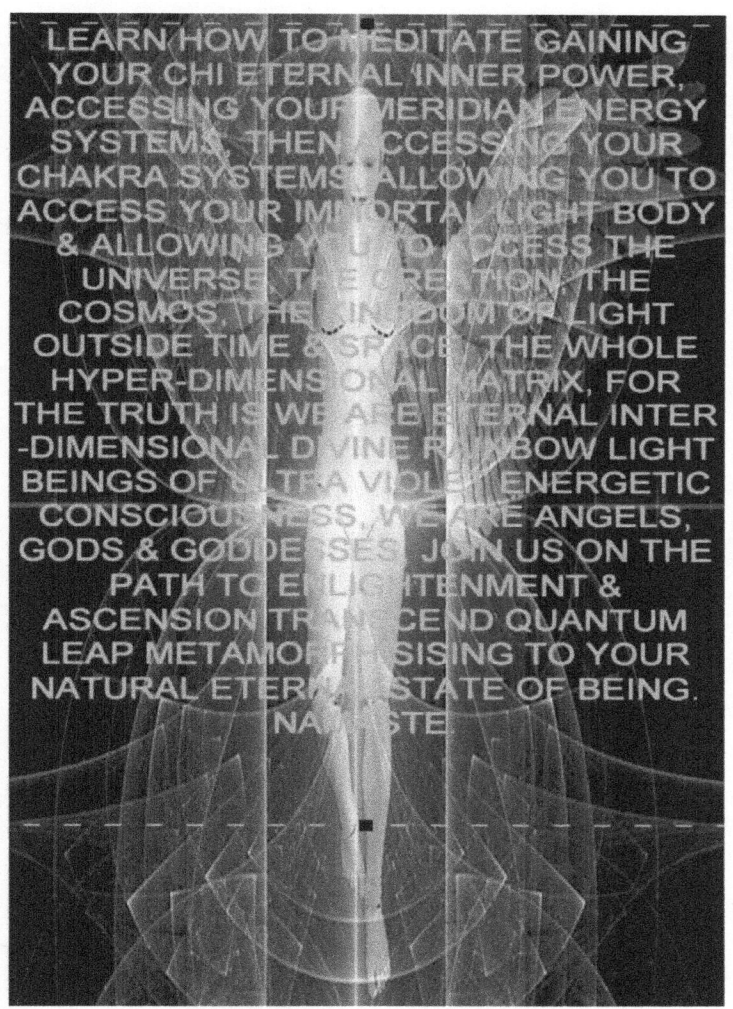

LEARN HOW TO MEDITATE GAINING YOUR CHI ETERNAL INNER POWER, ACCESSING YOUR MERIDIAN ENERGY SYSTEMS, THEN ACCESSING YOUR CHAKRA SYSTEMS, ALLOWING YOU TO ACCESS YOUR IMMORTAL LIGHT BODY & ALLOWING YOU TO ACCESS THE UNIVERSE, THE CREATION, THE COSMOS, THE KINGDOM OF LIGHT OUTSIDE TIME & SPACE, THE WHOLE HYPER-DIMENSIONAL MATRIX, FOR THE TRUTH IS WE ARE ETERNAL INTER-DIMENSIONAL DIVINE RAINBOW LIGHT BEINGS OF ULTRA VIOLET ENERGETIC CONSCIOUSNESS, WE ARE ANGELS, GODS & GODDESSES, JOIN US ON THE PATH TO ENLIGHTENMENT & ASCENSION TRANSCEND QUANTUM LEAP METAMORPHSISING TO YOUR NATURAL ETERNAL STATE OF BEING. NAMASTE

BACK COVER

MEDITATION THE KEY TO PEACEFUL MANIFESTATIONS

Meditation is the key to peaceful manifestations, then your inner peaceful thoughts will manifest outwards into vibratory words and actions, creating your physical reality of your choosing. Through stillness of the mind with breath work, and ancient breath practices, you will create space to have clarity. With clarity you will see the mind is just a tool of the human avatars, the human biological body in which we manifest, through the luminous energy field around around the human body, which is the software that informs the hardware the DNA to grow the body. The luminous energy field is a foot below your feet, a foot above your head and as wide as your arms stretch outwards.

Learn how to meditate gaining your chi eternal inner power accessing your meridian energy systems, then accessing your chakra systems allowing you to access your immortal light body and allowing you to access the universe, the creation, the cosmos, the kingdom of light outside time and space, accessing the whole hyper-dimensional matrix, for the truth is, we are eternal inter-dimensional divine rainbow light beings of ultra violet energetic consciousness we are angels, goddesses and gods. Please come join us on the path to enlightenment and ascension, transcend, quantum leap metamorphosing to your natural eternal state of being, namaste LoveLifeLee.

OTHER BOOKS BY LOVELIFELEE

FRONT COVER

BACK COVER

The Illusion of Rona The Maya of Demons The Royal Fallen Angel Bloodlines

The Illusion of Rona The Maya of Demons The Royal Fallen Angel Bloodlines, is a book written in the now 2020 as times are changing by force on society by criminal corrupt mentally ill evil people, that are in secret society cults, in a war part psychological on the human race, they come from ancient fallen angel bloodlines and there blackmailed puppet ministers in government and corporations that are lost in the minds of maya for greed power and control of the human race, this book discusses the illusion of reality created by these bloodlines and there agendas and there strategies forced on the masses still programmed from birth and then indoctrinated and brain washed into an illusion of reality and there weapons of choice used on society, like mind control, biological weapons as vaccines and illusion of false viruses and military grade microwave weapon systems, the poisoning of water, food, and the illusion of global warming, some of there history up to times in 2020 and there evil goals and the truth of our DNA makeup our bodies, consciousness and our light bodies and ascension.

This is an explosive and riveting compelling revealing book of ancient knowledge of the blueprint and schematics in your DNA to grow your eternal light body and this book reveals ancient knowledge of the fallen angels bloodlines the house of Saudi royals and the British German European royals of the Davidic Zionist Jewish orders from their Demonic Satanic Death Cult of Blood Sacrifice, their agendas including the Rona virus and use of military grade microwave frequency weapons and man made biological weapon virus vaccines and there psychological, physical and spiritual war on humanity of tyranny, for dominate complete control of society and the whole human race civilization. There intent to depopulate to a few hundred million and to imprison eternal souls manifesting here on earth by way of manipulating our DNA, so the human race cannot access higher levels of consciousness or the zero point energy field or the hyper-dimensional matrix of the creation, creating a slave race owned by corporations, trapped then in an eternal cycle of enslavement. An eye opener for many civilians especially if still under programming and indoctrination, of mind control.

Most importantly information on your DNA and your avatar your body about the blueprint and schematics to grow your light body and stop the cycles of life and death and ascend, and therefore not being trapped in this dimension of reality by Demons the

Archons the Jinn and the royal bloodlines they manifest into the Davidic Jewish orders of the satanic cult, also known as the illuminati, cabal and elite globalists.

These bloodlines are also known as the Kahazarian and Ashkenazi crime families that rule with brutal terror and genocide and perpetual murder assassinations to cover up these crimes on humanity.

1

INTRODUCTION

THE RECAPTURE OF THE REPUBLIC OF THE UNITED STATES BY A LONE U.S CITIZEN
BECOMING THE POST MASTER GENERAL OF THE WORLD

THE IMPLEMENTATION OF A NEW WORLDWIDE QUANTUM SYSTEM OF TRUTH RETURNING TO COMMON LAW OF THE LAND & A NEW STANDARD OF GOLD FOR COLLATERAL AS NO LONGER DO BIRTH CERTIFICES STAND.

So this part of the truth and facts are fascinating and it starts like this at this point in time in 1999, The

United States of America was very discreetly at that time, was being over taken from within by enemies foreign and domestic united to take over the USA, all the criminals were working for the English Monarch the King or Queen who reigns over a kingdom or an Empire, at the core of the empire is Great Britian, this plan has been in play for over Two Hundred years, and it was halted in its tracks, by one United States of America citizen, saving The United States Republic and the world from horrific horrors of control and Genocide.

So this one man a United States of America citizen named Russell Jay Gould, a true republican patriot, perceived what was happening, and about to take place, recognized the immediate and imminent threat, and took immediate action, recourse instantly acting to making use of persons and things for the aid in an effort to achieve, the saving of the Republic of The United States of America, with enthusiasm and viger and passion, he was on a mission to save his beloved republic for a patriot he truly be, and recognized for his effort and acheievements, may he rest in peace Amen, and be blessed eternally.

With a military style approach and specific strategic moves and plays he orchestrated the prevention of the take over of the United States of America and saved the Republic from being pillaged, plundered, overrun, invaded, stopped an invading force, so invasion by a foreign enemy and conquered, by the British Monarch of the Disgraced

Fallen Angel Royal desendants of the Goldsmith & Davidic Zionist Satanic Israelite Bloodlines.

This patriot went to the pentagon and took the situation in hand and used the legal regulations, there guide that operates the apparatus of the system to take the United States US TITLE No.4 Flag, with blessed permission the UNITED STATES TITLE FOUR FLAG was passed over to the patriot, and he resubmitted it to, and logged it into the United Nations, and used the same legal regulation at this corporate entity, corporate body, this then changed his Sovereignty Status, to the SOVEREIGN SUCCESSOR to QUEEN ELIZABETH the SECOND, so SOVEREIGN SUCCESSOR of Great Britian,what an absolute legend this patriot RUSSELL JAY

GOULD was, an absolute remarkable achievement in the face of adversity and other at times extreme adversity, and also repatented the US TITLE FOUR FLAG also in relation to the new quantum system of truth.

In time when things cooled down, he started taking control of several high ranking positions, taking Global Command, as (Director of the Federal Postal Judge), also as the (Joint Chief Federal Postal Judge), also as (Postal Inspector), also as (Post Master Bank Banker), also as (Vatican City Key Master), also as (World Central Bank Owner), also as (Prize Master), also as (Prize Commissioner), also as (Comptroller of the Global Foreign Postal Currency), also as (Post Master General), also as (Pentagon Pay

Master General), also as (Master Master General), also as (Muster Master Navy Commander & Chief – RUSSELL J GOULD).

Then that got the infiltraters of the republic attention and put them on notice, for commiting treason, so Criminal Terrorists and Satanists, and Geonocidal WAR CRIMINALS that have commited GENOCIDE on the whole collective humanities surface population.

2

THE INTRODUCTION OF A NEW QUANTUM CONSTRUCT A NEW LANGUAGE OF NOW TIME GRAMMER

This means that the Patriot of The Republic of The United States of America Russell Jay Gould, has introduced to The United States but also to the entire whole world, a new quantum construct a new language, a new grammer, so as he has put this in place it means he used this grammer and language of truth, to prove that all past financial and legal contracts – so documents to be fraudulent, so grammatical fraud had taken place worldwide and in The United States, so that meant monetary wise he saved the Republic of the United States trillions is depts as they were factually found to be false therefore fraudulent, of no value, null & void, not legally binding.

3

THE REDESIGNING OF THE PERIODIC TABLE OF ELEMENTS

Then this patriot had to redesign the periodic table of elements into a quantum construct, of truth, this man has aptitude and a strong passion for his inclination his action to save his republic and in doing so saved humanity and the world from one level of many levels, of one segment of the many segments, used by the dark, negative forces, human, and non-human their agendas, so Russell Jay Gould slowed the tranny, of the Fallen Angel Royal Disgraced descendant bloodlines, he is a genius, a true Patriot of The Republic of The United States of America.

4

THE NEW SOVEREIGN WORLD POST MASTER GENERAL RUSSEL JAY GOULD IS ILLEGALLY CRIMINALLY ARRESTED WITH NO LEGAL OR AUTHORITY TO DO SO

The arrest occurred because Russell Jay Gould, when he was taking sovereignty of the World Postal Master General and putting in place the new quantum system, he over looked one of the most important, and fundamental support aperatus, infrastructure and powers which was to inform the military on some of the steps he took, and so the criminal cabal the English infiltrators had there people inside the military so they were persuaded to stand down, I assume under duress by way of threats to life, or that of there families lifes, and the threat to wipe out your DNA genetic living breath realatives to murder your entire family, so no future of your bloodline will exist on the planet, there evil is despicable, but Universal Law of Karma shall be returned in full, by Universal Law of Attraction.

5

THE MORTGAGE COLLAPSE OF 2007 REVEALS ONE OF THE BIGGEST FRAUDS OF THE UNITED STATES AND THAT OF THE WORLD

The collapse of the morage industry in the United States of America at that time of the year 2007, this lead to investigations by many authorities, but one investigation by some in the military who had the right security cridentials the correct clearences, who were concerned about losing there properties, so united in a concerted manner to acertain, where this had stemmed from, the source of the issue or companies or persons at the core, of the original domino effect, that had orchestrated, the chains of events to cause the out come of the collapse of the United States of America mortgage industry in 2007.

So the investigative military unit after some months of time researching, found out about Russell Jay Gould and Judge David Wynn Miller, and there connection to the mortgage industry, that they were meant to be responsible for, because what they actually had done is syntaxed the entire global system, but able to keep it in its complete original state, so therefore in tact, in its original state but quantumtized the entire global system into a quantum true system, no fraud or deception can take place, a system fair to all citizens on earth and in law of the land, so common law of the living, breathing, of the living breathing woman or man, embodied on earth in the present, moment of now. They then realised that with the new quantum construct that the old legal contracts, so documents to be fraudulent, thus leading to all of The Republic of The United States to be considered free from the constrants of the illegal contracts therefore void of payment of any past depts to deptors, and past obligations in there entirety.

So the research the investigating unit had found was that Russell Jay Gould and David Wynn Miller that they were responsible for the mortgage industry and had syntaxed the morgages, finding grammatical fraud, so that means it was not the subprime mortgage lending that lead to the fall abruptly in the mortgage market, it was because Russell Jay Gould and David Wynn Miller had actually syntaxed the whole of the banking and morgage contracts, but by doing so it was found they were all grammatical fraud, because of this the companies holding them these contracts like Freddie Mac mortgage corporation and Fannie Mae bank realised this and packaged them and sold them immediately to, The Bank of America and then a few days later The Bank of America then realised what they had (paper contacts, failing to reach an acceptable standard, poor low quality morgage paper) and sold them all on to Wells Fargo bank, so this caused the swift sales of these spoiled morgages happening rapidly to started the collapse of the mortgage industry in the year 2007.

6

THE SYNTAX KEY

So the investigative unit looked into these two gentlemen, patriots of the republic, then the parts came together to unlock the whole puzzle of what had occurred, that was that they found a grammer key on the morgages that had been syntaxed, so they had a syntax key which is a grammer key, stamped on the side of the mortgage contract document paperwork, so many people believe that grammer and syntax are the same concepts but while both dictate the construct of a sentence, is is much more accurate to say that syntax is actually one part of grammer, there are many rules this is known as grammer, but creating the structural frame of the sentence is known as syntax.

So grammer is the set of rules a language uses to convey meaning, it is one of the fundamental building blocks of language, along with lexicon or vocabulary, so that means when you use proper grammer you are following generally accepted rules of your language.

So the elements of the grammer include – Morphology, the ways morphemes connect to make words, then comes, Phonology, the sounds of words, then comes, Semantics, the meanings of words and relationships between words, then comes Syntax, the structure of words in a sentence.

Grammer dictates the ways you use words especially parts of sound, so speech, for example, nouns and verbs must agree with each other in your sentence, but the order words are in that sentence relies on its Syntax, so structure, the frame work.

Elements of syntax which means arrange together, and syntax has more to do with linguistics than language, because syntax is part of grammer all syntactical rules are also the grammer rules, the elements of syntax are –

Parts of a Sentence, subject, predicate, object, direct object, then the Phrases, a group of words without a subject or predicate, then the Clauses, a group of words with a subject and verb, then the Sentence Structure, the construction of simple, compound, complex, or compound-complex sentences.

Grammer rules and patterns dictate the ways you use the syntactical parts of a sentence, for example every sentence must include a subject and a predicate, but while there are basic syntactic rules to follow, syntax makes it possible for writers to establish tone by varying the types of sentences in their writing.

Every sentence you read and say, so speak follows the rules of grammer and syntax, even when you use informal or colloquial speech, you are following a syntactical pattern that best conveys your meaning to your friends and peers.

Then the investigating unit understood how this syntax system worked and understood the fraud that was occurring, but they still had to work out what gave the syntax key that was stamped on the mortgage contracts the power or authority to actually syntax these documents, at this point when the investigating unit discovered the truth it was found to be the biggest national security secret of all time in The United States and that of the Entire World.

So several avenues of enquiry were opened up, one leading to the going back in time to the beginning of The United States Republics history, to understand and solve this avenue of enquiry they had to research and trace information, documentation back to the start of the thirteen colonies.

IT WAS FOUND THAT THE WORD AMERICA, WHEN BROKEN DOWN USING THE NEW QUANTUM GRAMMER SYSTEM OF NOW TIME TRUTH GRAMMER, the codes/the meaning of AMERICA acutally meant-
A – Latin for No
MERI – is Latin for Mercy
CA – means Sheep
AMERICA – NO MERCY FOR THE SHEEP!!!!!!!!!!!!!

This example above reminds me of one of my other books The Royal Cults Covens Language of Spells, this book explains about language and its use and context in statue law and admiralty law, and how your vocalised words communicate to you tetrahedron sacred gemometric building blocks that build the structure of the cells of your biological human avatar manifesting matter into being and other knowledge of the scaffolding of life and of the schematic blueprint instructions in your DNA to grow your eternal light body.

7

TRACING THE HISTORY OF THE REPUBLIC OF THE UNITED STATES OF AMERICA

This all starts really back in time when the thirteen colonies got to the point they went into bankruptcy, so it all starts with the first bankruptcy of the United States of America's Republic, at the time the thirteen colonies were fighting for their freedom from the tyrant the King of England the British Crown, at this time there was a post office in Philadelphia this was named The Benjamin Franklin Post Office and was open for business until the war commenced, this is because all war voids all contracts.

The thirteen colonies at this time were not an independent state of there own, or a nation of there own, so therefore the thirteen colonies had to shut shop, shut down the the Benjamin Franklin Post Office in Philadelphia, this is because at the time they were fighting for the national statehood, so fighting a nation state a territorially bound sovereign polity a state of citizenship, political organization, constitution of state, administrative direction, to bring into harmony, so to act in accordance to the agreed conform of rules, that is ruled in the name of a community of citizens who identify themselves as a Nation.

8

THE END OF THE AMERICAN REVOLUTION

When the American revolution was over the Philidelphia Benjamin Franklin Post Office was no longer able to resume business as it had now gone into bankruptcy, it actually owed one million six hundred thousand francs to France for lending the money to pay for and start the

American revolution, at this time France and spain got into a verbal battle over which nation was going to put there nations Post Master in the General position in the colonies of the United States Republic Colonies to control commerce and open the post office back up for business to receive tax payments for there nations, from the movement of goods in the colonies. From Frances point of view they had loaned the money the one million six hundred thousand francs to finance the revolution so therefore felt they had the right to place a French Post Master General in the thirteen colonies of America.

From Spains point of view they argued that Christopher Columbus found the lands of America first therefore this entitled Spain to take position of Post Master General.

Then came on the scene the King of England, The King of Great Britain who was the worlds reigning monarch at that point in time, the King of England communicated to France and Spain that he was the reigning monarch of the world and so he was putting his post office in the American colonies with an English Post Master General in place, as the citizens of the American colonies were considered his people, so he did just that.

9

THE FOUNDERS OF THE REPUBLIC

When you go back to the time the founders founded the republic you find that they discussed this and spoke of that they would prefer to have the king of England as the post master of the Americas as they did not know the ways of the French or Spanish monarchs and would rather deal with the devil they knew, and they knew how that british monarch operated, so they continued to work with the king of England as they knew how his construct of commerce worked. So the Great Britan post office was placed and located in Washington D.C, which is actually a Foregin entity of the United States and should never of had been truthfully been a part of the United States of America, so it is a part of a territory of a state that is enclosed within the territory of another state or nation, so it has never ever been a part of the United States of America it was opened up for business, as a District of Columbia as a foreign onclave, the reason being it was the post office for Great Britan, meaning the King of England, the King of Great Britan locating his post office in the Americas could now be open for business to the world and start allowing trading commerce to be conducted, so that as reigning monarch if other nation monarchs wanted to come and trade in the Americas they had to pay him a tax,

by doing this it stops the pillaging of the nations resources, the tax payments including any goods trading commerce in the America that arrives by shipping from any nation, all tax payments would have to pass through the English Kings Great Britan Post Office.
So this was the First Bankrupcy of the United States of America, when Benjamin Franklin borrowed one million six hundred thousand francs from France, for the revolution.

10

THE GENTLEMENS AGREEMENT BROKEN BY ABRAHAM LINCOIN

So that meant the First bankruptcy of the United States of America was when Benjamin Franklin borrowed money from the French of one million six hundred thousand francs for the financing of the revolution. Historic record shows the Founding Fathers had agreed on a pact a gentlemens accord which was an agreement between themselves to Never borrow any money from the IMF World Banks, the reason they agreed this is because the IMF world banks do not owe aligence to any sovereignty, or to any particular monarch, they are an entity, or entities, so private bodies, conducting commerce, business of there own rules, regulations.

So what the Founding Fathers accord, the gentlemens agreement came to, was that they would only ever borrow money from other monarchs, this is because a monarch is only as powerful as the size and strength of there navies, armies, so therefore this meant to play the smart move was to be in contract with two different monarchs at the same time, this would limit the chances of one or the other monarchs invading the Americas, because if a foregin monarch was going to make war, with the Americas it had to communicate with the other monarch doing business, so trade commerce, with the other monarch, as if a war is started this means all Contracts would become void, and the other monarch would loss all there investment and trade in commerce on a huge scale a massive financial loss, this play would give time to the American colonies to get a plan and get organised if they were going to be invaded.

So Benjamin Franklin, he borrowed one million six hundred thousand francs from the French, for the financing of the revolution, so this was the start cause of the first bankruptcy and the effect, huge debt, and the King of England as Post Master General of the United States of America.

So then we come to Abraham Lincoin he started the cause of the effect of the Second United States bankruptcy he broke the agreement to never borrow money, so as not to allow the republic to become debtors so no control could be exerted over the republic, as the Founding

Fathers had agreed on a pact a gentlemens accord which was an agreement between themselves to Never borrow any money from the IMF World Banks, the reason they agreed this is because the IMF world banks do not owe aligence to any sovereignty, or to any particular monarch, they are an entity, or entities, so private bodies, conducting commerce, business of there own rules, regulations.

So then breaking the agreement never to borrow money for the Republic from private banks, Abraham Lincoln put the United States in debt by borrowing money from the World IMF Bank, because after the Civil War, Abraham Lincoln had after the colonies were dissolved and the colonies split in two, at that time there was no United States it had dissolved, you had the south against the north considered to be to disconnected, separated, parted countries, that were at war with each over, in battles all over the Americas lands, but the south did actually raise there flag and in doing so they established its self as a republic of its own South nation state.

Then we see that Abraham Lincoin broke the ForeFathers accord the gentlemens agreement, which is a treasonous act in its self, by borrowing money from IMF world bank completely disregarding and violating the ForeFathers accord the gentlemens agreement.

So when Abraham Lincoin commited this treasonous act, the cause he started with the loan and the effect was the start of the Second International Bancruptcy of The United States of America. That leads to the year 1933 to the start of the third, so final international bankruptcy of the United States of America, this is when the stock market began to crash causing the depression that happened in 1929, so this the sequence of especially significant occurrences layed out are the cause and effect of the three bankruptcies of the United States of America.

11

RELATION TO THE MORGAGES STAMPED WITH SYNTAX KEY AUTHORITY

So whole history of the United States of America had to be researched and all historic documents thoroughly and meticulously investigated to come to the conclusion and to ascertain the origin of the syntax key stamps on the mortgage documents of the 2007 mortgage fall, collapse.

So the investigating unit could ascertain what gave power to the syntax key the stamp on and over the mortgage documents, to be used so utilised on the mortgage contracts, so by what authority, to use the syntax in the customary mode of acting in the manner it was conducted in, to direct the course of and manage control over, so have power and ultimate authority and sovereignty and validation of these documents as fraudulent, so the authority to validate the documents were void because of grammical fraud, banking fraud.

So when the investigating unit understood the syntax keys authority were it came from and how the contracting it conducted by way of stamping the mortgage documents, it was at that point the realization that the biggest secret had been hidden in the United States of America, the largest national security threat the nation has ever faced and the most hugest world wide fraud, grammer fraud of all world wide legal documents, along with banking fraud and other frauds also.

12

THE BIRTH CERTIFICATE FRAUD

Leads down the path to birth certificate fraud, how the birth certificate was created, it was because the United States went into bankruptcy 9th march 1933, so citizens were used as collateral instead of gold at that time, so The United States of

America could keep the economy going, then started to take out loans from private banks that were not affiliated with any governments, which was a corporation called the Federal Reserve.

The United States of American had no money to pay back the loans to the private corporation the Federal Reserve, so thay used the citizens labour as collateral, so this was the commence of the beginning of the third and final bankruptcy of the United States of America, as the they owed vast amounts of money in debts to the IMF world banks all because President Abraham Lincoln had commited treason by resorting to the world banks, breaking the agreement the accord the ForeFathers of The Republic of the United States of America had put in place, as the caution to not be indebted to the IMF world banks, and then inturn that they could have power exerted over the United States of America and its citizens, aware this could lead to enslavement.

Then we come to President Franklin D. Roosevelt, who had to yield control of possession and surrender all of the United States of Americas Gold Reserves and hand them over to the Criminal IMF world bank to cover the debts owed from the loans, at this time the United States of America had no more specified resources, so declared to be bankrupt the legal process through which people or other entities who cannot repay debts to creditors may seek relief from some or all of their debts, normally in most jurisdictions imposed by a court order often initiated by the debtor in this case the IMF world bank.

The United States of America had no cash flow this is why the BIRTH CERTIFICATE system of enslavement was set up, they used citizens energy of labour as collateral, so the citizens were used as the collateral instead of Gold Bars. This is why taxes were placed on the people to pay of the outstanding owed debts of the loans The United States of Ameica had to pay off to the Criminal

IMF banks, and also to pay any debts that would occur in the rebuilding ecomomically and for all other infrastructure a nation needs to be in commerce, so business and costs of security that The United States of America needed in the future.

The WORLD NEEDS TO KNOW this corrupt criminal fraudulent system came crashing down and collapsed and ceased to be in existence in the year and date of the 2nd of November 1999, its know that this secret has been kept because the criminals that have infiltrated the United States of America government and most worldwide governments, known by many names they are The Cabal, The Seven Orders, The illuminati, The Deep State, The Shadow Government.

13

THE MILITARY IS TAKING DOWN CRIMINAL INFILTRATORS BEHIND THE SHADOW GOVERNMENT

These criminals that have infiltrated the United States of America governments and the world, known by many names The Cabal, The Seven Orders, The illuminati, The Deep State, The Shadow Government. They are one and the same they are the Fallen Angel Descendants, the Disgraced British German European, Royal bloodlines of the Goldsmith Davidic Zionist Israelite Demonic Satanic cult orders, (the other Royal bloodlines are The House of Saud) that worship the Canaanite deity BAAL (Lord), known also Moloch associated with child sacrifice, blood consumption, blood practices and ceremonies of the dark arts of negative magicians and witches, so they are the thirteen families of the Satanic Cult Orders that worship Lucifer.

So this is why the secret has been kept so long as they keep power by blackmail, threat of death, your families deaths, or your entire bloodlines to be assasinated, controlling through fear and intimidation, but at this time beyond the world citizens view the military is conducting world wide operations to take down these pedophile child sacrificing Genocidal WAR CRIMINALS, and arrests are

happening out of the publics view as not to alarm the public, so they are conducting military trials behind closed doors, as they know the citizens will want to hunt them down when there sick crimes of children, of humanity as a whole and genocide, so the military will be revealing this in the near future.
Then the monies, gold, silver that was stolen from world citizens the wealth from these criminals, there resources will be confliscated and returned to world citizens to start afresh rebuilding all nations infrastructer and economies and the hidden advanced technologies will be revealed and avalible for healing, energy and so much more.
So at this point the military know who they are how they operate, but there has been military insiders collecting data on them for over 70 years collecting intelligence and the National Security Agency has collected data for the last fifthteen years they have all the evidence, the NSA have tracked all the elicit wealth in the world, they know that absolutally

without a shadow of a doubt that wall street has stolen over a one hundred trillion dollars from the people, the worldwide citizens, from society, just another one of the secrets kept by these crimminals, they stole this money, the peoples wealth by NAKED SELLING, SHORT SELLING, wall street has also laundered over one hundred trillion dollars in corrupt dirty money from trafficking in children, women, human beings, gold, silver, drugs legal and illegal on the black market, and guns and other weapons, this evidence is being used at this time to take them down, they have them with there heads in the noose they cannot survive this they have only one option which is that there only out is to turn informer immediately and get a reduced sentence only if there crimes aren't to do with the satanic practices, of children or murder, they have to give the truth and reconciliation and make a deal or they will be put to death, for War Criminal acts of crimes TREASON, crimes of humanity so GENOCIDE, by military courts with swift sentences to be carried out.

The intellegengence services and infrastructure does not serve the people it serves these criminals the shadow government, the CIA The Central Intelligence agency had been commiting crimes of humanity by way of rendition, torture, assassination, drone assassination, regime changes in other governments, doing operations to set up and start wars that are always based on lies, deceit, the reason being is because all of these criminal organizations gain huge financial profit from trafficking in humans, weapons and drugs legal and illegal, this all leads back to the shadow government who control this criminal empire and also wall street.

So THE WAR IS HAPPENING AND HAS FOR YEARS BUT ESCILATING UNDER GROUND IN THE D.U.M.B.S deep under ground bases in the entire system, so an UNDER EARTH WAR is RAGING at this time, which really truthfully is the PROLONGED SPIRITUAL WAR FOR THE SURVIVAL of EDEN PLANET EARTH & HUMANITY.

You must realize that Our Struggle is not against the Flesh and Blood, but against the Rulers, against the Authorities, against the Power of this Dark World and against the SPIRITUAL FORCES of EVIL in the Heavenly Realms.

There are Four Stages of this Prolonged Spiritual Battle between Good & Evil or the Evil Darkness Forces that stand opposed to the DIVINE PLAN of The One True Living God & those that have dedicated themselves to the Service of The One True Living God, that is you and me in the State of God Consciousness connected to all eternal in the oneness of creation, Namaste.

The four stages necessary to complete in order to Win this War against Evil Darkness that descended centuries ago on to our Gaia Planet Mother Earth, Pachamama & attacked Humanity Viscously, Ferociously, Savagely with the Satanc Demonic energy with Ferocity of Intense Extreme Cruelty. The Four Stages are as follows –

One – Remove the Evil Darkness fron The Space about the Planet Earth and maintain Permanent Supremacy there in that space.

Two – Remove the Evil Darkness from Earth's Skies and maintain Permanent Supremacy there in that space.

Three – Remove the Evil Darkness from the Surface of the Planet Earth and maintain Permanent Supremacy there in that space.

Four – Remove the Evil Darkness from the Beneath the surface of the Planet Earth (in the underground bases and cities there are over One Hundred & Thirty One Underground cities connected to each other in the United States alone, worldwide over One Thousand & Four Hundred), throughout all th underground Tunnels, Labyrinths, Caverns, Larva tubes, & DUMBS & maintain Permanent Supremacy there in those spaces.

So the draining and removal of the Satanic Evil Upper Echelon is proceeding and within in all branches of these countries and governments, the arrests, trials, sentencing is happening it appears Guantanomo Bay Prison has been expand and is housing famous stars, politicians, the disgraced bloodline family members, its said some may have been put to death already executed for TREASON, sentenced by military as there crimes are Unconprehendable, Satanic in nature.

14

THE BIRTH CERTICICATE SYSTEM
THE VATICAN & CITY OF LONDON

The birth certificate system uses the citizens as collaternal to create an income off of there labour, the peoples energy, to substanciate to support the wealth that was nessecery to go a head and to return to the needed actual level of rebuilding that economy and the authentication validation comfirmation of administrative needs to that which areas a United States of America Nation need to have in place. So then you start to perceive that the birth certificate system is connected to the most hugest, biggest warfare platform on earth in the entire world, this system was orchestrated by the fallen angel disgraced royal bloodlines to enslave and capture every world citizen, to be used as chattle meaning a chattel person an item of movable personal property, such as furniture, domestic animals, or human beings in this case. They implemented this plan to create wealth off other beings hard labour to build there empire and to doinate with no mercy there supposed chattle, they are parasites of the worst kind, consuming our energy and literally feeding of our children and our blood. The birth certificate system leads back to the Vatican and of course another strong hold of the royal bloodlines the city of London and to the Pentagon Complex, these were the three main war command bases of the criminals, that substanciated the empire of the three city states.

The Vatican practices the conducting of esoteric doctrines and the symbolism they use and operate with behind the entire warfare platform, its full of esoteric symbols and ancient knowledge, looking down at the Vatican stronghold compound you perceieve a falise, key hole and paths representing the timelines and shipping commerce lanes from the centre of the key hole, to door ways that lead from those time lines and shipping commerce lanes, the falise in the centre represents the female womb, then around the top of the key hole circumference building are stone statues of males, this represents the males all in line waiting there turn to do disapproving, bad, harmful activity to the world and its citizens, to cause pain, suffering and destruction. This means at the Vatican they are the evil neagative ones waiting for there turn to being in the top position power of the sitting pope, so they can be in charge of the business this cult operates, runs and practices, from the Vatican, as we know it is its own state and bank, an independent sovereignty to its self. So they claim to being in charge of TIME, this warfare platform was a location on planet earth to capture time, this is in symbolism at the Vatican where there are gargoials statues holding the sands of time horizontally which is to stop the sand from flowing down and up, so meaning that they had captured time with the gregorian calendar.

15

TRUTH OF THE GREGORIAN CALENDAR WARFARE PLATFORM

So the Vatican is not what it appears to be or represent, this is not the house of God or Christians for there has be subversion for there has been an illusion of the truth for fallen angel descendants and others non-humans practice dark magic, blood ceremonies, child sacrifice this is the disgraced royal bloodlines cult, one of strong hold of there grip over humanity. The audience hall in the Vatican city is representing a reptilian in its shape architecture and décor, that shows the truth a homage to the Draco reptilians that are from the Draco star system.

All HUMANITIES past and present problems manifested because back thousands of years ago at Atlantean times supposedly the elite priests were using pyramid technology carelessly or intentionally, and opened up a space time continuum allowing a porthole to open and the Draco came through and they genetically messed with humanity to Enslave us in Time and they turned Ten of our Twelve Strands of DNA OFF, leaving us operating and functioning on only Two strands of DNA, leaving us in a DUALITY REALITY, this where the troubles started and began for our species on earth our race of humanity.

This is why you have millions of these fallen star children the illuminati luciferian Satanist ancient Babylonian of the mystery schools, freemason esoteric occult , the New Age cult leaders teaching the most programmed, indoctrinated then brain washed human species populace of their Satan Luciferian Atlantean old paradigm deception doctrines of extraterrestrials and extraterrestrial channeling which in truth is demon spirit channeling sittings. They are a mix of Extratrestrials in human avatars and the Jinn the Archons the 4th, 5th density beings with no physical form and they manifest into clones human avatars, these are the negative entities so energies of Satan, Demons, Devils the energy of Lucifer.

So the Vatican was the place on earth representing the location on earth that has captured Time, so with the Gregorian calender its them that tell us what day of the week that it is Monday, Tuesday, Wednesday, Thursday, Friday, Saturday, Sunday, this is the calender that all the stock markets are dictated by, and use to payout the percentage of corporate earnings that is paid dividends to shareholders, the recipients receives of investments, so this means all of the commerce and shipping of goods moves by this calender, so the Vatican purpose to watch all movement of commerce and shipping, remember the Vatican city has its own bank also being its own sovereignty, the Vatican claims it has been given heavenly authorizations which absolute rubbish, a fabrication, false, a lie, to be in control of and in command of these shipping lanes of commerce, and the time lines so they can observe the movement of shipping and all commerce of cargo, this means in monitary terms they watch over all movement of planet earths money, this includes the movement of all civilian and worldwide militaries as if you follow the money for supplies, you know all militaries worldwide movements, so the Vatican has known whos behind the wars and who starts the wars and when the wars will conclude, finish, stop.

16

THE END OF THE THIRD & FINAL UNITED STATES OF AMERICA BANCRUPTCY

The end of the third bankruptcy was on the 2nd of November 1999, so this meant that the post office that had been opened for commerce at the out laying portion of country surrounded by the territory of another country the enclave of Washington District of Columbia, so the king of England had to leave so vacate his position as Post Master Commander so his post office was closed and so it was closed for commerce, no tax payments, so the president of The United States in the past was always the Aministrator trustee, so therefore Aminstrator for the bankruptcy, so now that the final third bankruptcy had occurred the Kings post office was forced to close doors and shut shop, stop all tax of trade and commerce, because this was the end of the bankruptcy there therefore was not a need for a trustee any longer.

You have to understand that this is a War the War Great Britan has waged on the Republic of The United States of America for a couple of hundred years, this was the United Kingdoms long term plan, the goal to infiltrate the Republic and to get in high powerful positions in government, and in corporations and take over from within, this is a long rage time frame Warfare Strategy, by the King of England and his Descendants have followed his warfare plan out up to this day, infiltrated The Republic of The United States of America and reeked havoc destruction on the world and devastated and genocided humanity, all cultures, races, Karma they will have to pay, Law of Attraction, Universal Law, Karmic Law, but at the end of the day they are us, for we are one in the oneness of creation, this we come to learn when woken up consciously, to the make up of life, the universe, the hyperdimensional matrix, the realities inside and outside of time, where the eternal realms are and the Immortal Kingdom of Light resides, we learn the energies involved to create matter, so structured life with intention of love light and create magic and wonder in our manifested true nature of an eternal embodied immortal divine angelic light being, in a human avatar, magical in nature life be, as we weave webs of light into the fabric of time and space, for goddesses and god creaters we be of divine chi light energy, awesome.

Now we come back to the Kings future generations knowning that the United States could not pay the debtors, the IMF world bank, because of the interest rates were high, as this originally occurred when Abraham Lincoin broke the ForeFathers accord and borrowed from the IMF world bank and incurred the huge debts, so at the time of the bankruptcy the King of the future descendants of the Old past King would intervene and the King would pay the debt to th IMF world bank and be Ruler, King of the Republic of The United States of America, that would now be under Great Britians authority, to be used as chattle, reduced to serves, slaves and peseants. That did not happen as the Postoffice shut down and the King had to vacate his position.

17

A TWENTY DAY WINDOW TO SAVE THE REPUBLIC OF THE UNITED STATES OF AMERICA

The Washington District of Columbia Post office had not closed down but the king had to vacate at this point in time he vacated there was an eighteen day window open at the post office, enough time to save the Republic, this is where Russell Jay Gould and David Wynn

Miller comes to rescue of The Republic and in doing so the world from certain agendas against worldwide citizens.
So Russel J Gould went immediately to the Pentagon Building and asked them if they had a copy right patent on the Title Four Flag of The UNITED STATES, the reply was they had not had anyone ask this before, he explained what was happening The United States of America was about to be over taken and captured by the King of England and Great Britan, and told them that he had syntaxed the Title Four Flag of The United States anyway and disqualified the old one due to grammer fraud. Russell Jay Gould told them that as a citizen of the Republic of The United States of America he had the right to stand up for and guard, to protect the Republic of the American Nation, so he must protect the Title Four Flag, from enemies domestic and foreign, so he takes hold and embraces clasping the Title Four Flag in his arms, now he has it in his possesssion he goes directly to the United Nations, were he enrolls the flag, so

registered and catalogued, they ask him which land was to be catalogued as all the land in the world is taken, so he replyed he would be taking or registering the Land of the Courts, which are the ports, during the time of the contract, so this gave Russell Jay Gould the most powerful position in the world in the most powerful highest court in the world, so this gave Russell Jay Gould the most powerful position in the world in the most powerful court on planet earth, so then after that he still had time spare in the eighteen day vacancy of the King of England and in turn Great Britan, so at this point he now goes back and registers as Post Master General of the United States of America and in doing so becomes the Worlds Post Master General, Russell Jay Gould also keeps the Post office open for commerce to still continue and allow business to be conducted but now under his authority, and keeps the continuence of the evidence so that of record documented, this means the Post office was no longer under the authority of the King, so no longer under Great Britans authority, what a legend a true patriot of the Republic, that being the case he succeeded as the sovereign from Great Britan after Queen Elizabeth the Second, this was because the United Nations gave him sovereginty status when he registered the land of the courts, so this gave him the power and authority to authorise the continued induction the act of inducting into office and the conduction allowing the flow of commerce through substance, in The Republic of The United States of America.

18

THE UNITED STATES MILITARIES THE NAVY

So at this time this meant the The United States of Americas military the navy was located in worldwide positions some in foreign ports in war ships, with no nation state country as there governing body, so no country at this moment in time, because russell Jay Gould has possession of the Title Four Flag so the navy does not have a flag to operate under, this is all catalogued and registered in the presidential documented paperwork in the congressional records.

At this time the now known rapist and pedophile the disgraced Bill Clinton the President of The United States of America at that time was with the National Security Council and was in foreign lands in Europe, in the country Kosavo in the Balkens region of Europe, first thing in the morning he received a telephone communication that was from inside The United States of America comfirming to the president that the Title Four Flag of The United States of America had been taken and held so captured and was now in the procession and control by Russell Jay Gould and David Wynn Miller, and the president was informed that its was now their registered flag and that they had sovereignty over its full command and control, also he was informed that they had prevented and stopped the take over and capture of The United States of

America, by the orchestrated long time framed military operation of over two hundred years, the warfare attack strategy implemented by the King of England, so therefore prevented the take over to Great Britan.

This meant the navy then straight away signed up and registered with Russell Jay Gould in 2003 agreeing he was in the new power of being the sovereignty of the United States of America Nation, you are in poccession of the new patented United States Titled Four Flag and we recognise you saved The Republic of The United States of America Nation from being captured and so they registered and swore in with him, and as no one man had ever saved the Republic in its history as this great respected Patriot had achieved, its quite a remarkable feat that he took on this endever for his passion for the Republic and he acheived his mission with full success, just absolutely remarkable is the gentlemen that is Russell Jay Gould and so is David Wynn Miller also another great Patriot of the

Republic of The United States of America.

So then Russel J Gould could then release the United States flag to the navy to fly on there ships this meant the navy could now continue to carry out its duties to the United States and its commerce and shipments, this is of course because the business of the navy is all concerned with the maritime practices of shipping and Protection and security of shipping lanes as well as boarders, so they could then continue to move around the world to protect the United States of America in an offensive or defensive position depending on the circumstances of the real time situations of the navies security and defense duties.

So this meant Russell J Gould entered the position of Commander and Chief of The North American continent so that includes The United States of America and Canada. This leads back to the Post Master General position he took over of the United States as it also governs Canada as its attached to that location via the post offices, therefore Russell Jay Gould took over as the Canadian Post Office Master General, of the Canadian post offices, so therefore he was now in the position and control of the whole entire North American continent, what a legend many smart plays, well orchestrated.

19

THE UNITED STATES OF AMERICAS CONSTITUTION WAS IT IN PERIL

So was there a point in time the United States of America constitution was at exposure to the risk of loss, in danger, in jeopardy of being over turned and destroyed, the administration in Washington District of Columbia, informed that the constitution was dissolved but not The United States of America Constitution in relation to the Bill of Rights, The Freedoms, the legistrative operations of the government, the executive and the judistal branch, so it was not the actual United States of America Constitution that dissolved, it was in relation to the banking constitution that had dissolved, this is what had constituted the United States of America, so the outline for the banking constitution had come to a time that these contracts had ceased to exist, ended in there entirety, because of the end of the third and final bankruptcy of the United States of America, so this meant there was not a need any more for a trustee that usually was the President of The United States of America, this meant at this time it was crucial to reestablish a new governance, so to reconsolidate and resubstanciate the entire nation, to reorganize and set up new Senate of the upper chambers of congress and house representatives of the lower chambers to constitute the legislature of The United States of

America at the capital building in Washington District of Columbria, so choose new congress members, and elect a new President to over see the nations and people needs and security, and go through the process of reconstruction of the Republic of The United States of America to go in the direction of momentum in the new constructed Quantum system, of course because Russell Jay Gould has put in place the New Quantum Gloabal system of truth in true Now Time grammer, so all future contracts are in quantum form of true grammer, this is the first time on earth that its been introduced and this quantum system cuts our fraud, so removes corruption with this new quantum construct.

So you need to recognize it was not the end of the United States of Americas constitution where it comes to the peoples liberties and laws it was only the end of the banking constitution in its entirety, because it was the time of the end of the third and final bankruptcy of The United States of America, this also means that the birth certificate system collapsed and ended in The United States of America. This means that all the United States citizens children that were born after the 2nd of November 1999 were never meant to be registered under this illegal birth certificate fraudulent corrupt system, which is a vicious and villainous in nature a criminally conducted operation of deceit and control carrying the energy of Luficer, that was the aim of this birth certificate enslavement system.

20

PERCEIVING THE ENSLAVEMENT OF BIRTH CERIFICATE SYSTEM

You have to learn to understand what the birth certificates are truly about as when you draw breath on this planet Gaia our Mother Earth, Pachamama she be also known as, so when you are born into this world and your birth mother delivers you and you draw breath, you are told that you must sign a document, which is called a birth certificate, before you leave the hospital of medical center with your new born child your infant baby, or they say you can't leave with your infant new born baby, so therefore you are entering your child into contract , well you do not have to sign your child into a birth certificate contract, the lie is a fiction, trickery, to deceive you into signing your child into slavery. Its insane to say you can't leave a medical facility or hospital with your child if you don't sign a peace of paper a document, which we now know to be fraudulant, this is a silent form of unlawful seizure and detention of a child, a grave and considered a highly criminal grave offense, usually punishable by long prison sentences or death, so an unlawful fraudulent birth certificate criminal system that was and is commiting the act of legal kidnapping, but really illegal kidnapping of children worldwide. Its just crazy absolute madness, that if you don't sign a document they feel they can take your infant away from you, no one has the sovereignty or right to take another eternal beings living breathing human infant baby from them, end of just insanity.

So when a mother signs the birth certificate system with the childs first name and last name it is in the print of Capital Letters meaning a ficticious entity that does not exist a fictional character that is not living breathing in physical form, so the infants name in capital letters and your birth mother signs in cursive, which is actually considered to be an necromancy which means the conjouring of souls of the dead meaning communication with the dead.

When you research you see that the only other places you see Capital letters on anyones name is on a tomb stone, as you are now a none breathing physical being you have left your avatar and passed back to another dimension, so you are classified as a a dead person a dead entity. So this means when you manifest into a human avatar biological body and are born you are therefore considered a

Dead Entity, because of the shipping wars that we are in, from the warfare platorm waged upon humanity, insane madness, negative magic of an illusion from the dark magicans, of the embodied demons, devils the Jinn and the Archons and negative extraterrestrials in human avatars, black magic therefore this is the trickery of sorcery from the lucifian cult, by deception of language grammer which is fraudulent in nature in conception.

This is a way by of therefore exerting the means to exert control over human beings over the civilisation of humanity to entrap through deceit and trickery into slavery, by way of the shipping wars, so when your birth mother signs the document she signs in cursive so therefore with out her knowledge and consent she is unawre she is conducting necromancy, as we know communicating with the dead, and when you are contracted into this huge apparatus machine warfare shipping commerce platform, the corporated actual construct of this vast empire of the fallen

angels descendants that operate and control the three most powerful world wide states the Vatican, The City of London and The Pentagon.
So you are regarded in this birth certificate system your considered automatically in there intended premeditated by tactical fashion to be missing, lost at sea or presumed dead, so your considered a piece of merchandise, goods or cargo, the property owned by another, a serve, a slave of energy.

21

THE SEVEN SECRET ORDERS
&
SECRET LOGDGES OF EARTH CONTROL SYSTEM

These old orders and secret societies operate from the three city strongholds and control all commerce and shipping and all monitary associated with this worldwide global Luciferian network of complete control and dominance, ruthlessly with out mercy, the Vatican and there roll played and the power of the esoteric symbolism that's used by these ancient negative orders of The Knights of Lazarus, The Knights of Columbus, The Knights of Malta, The Knights of Hospitaller, The Teutonic Knights, The Order of Saint James, The Order of Calatrava, The Knights of Templar the Vaticans order of assasins the Jesuits the Rothschilds family bloodlines Order. These are the private armies the mercinaries for the Vatican the ruthless enforcers, these are the secret societies of lodges of the fallen angel descendant bloodlines, this is just another mechinisim of how they have dominated control fantatically over the planet earth and enslaved and manipulated and controlled humanity as a whole civilization. This is why the warfare platform of the timeline and shipping lanes is so important to the fabric of there structured control of dominance and manipulation, and they utilize this command structure and implemented this particular system, to control wealth as to gain there personal wealth again dominating humanity by taking, actually stealing or robbing world citizens blindly on a continuum, so eventually in there warfare strategy to have the worlds people impoverished and to be dependant on the state for food, housing and income therefore in a communist fascist dictatorship in smart cities.

So back to the birth certificates they perceive you as property chattle owned, but we know this is a fictitious so fabricated entity not breathing living so therefore not you, its just an illegal fraudulent document contract they try to make you to agree to contract via trickery of capital grammer via illegal statue corporate law, law of contracts, a criminal scamming corrupt system.

So you are considers freight and so owned but who claims ownership of humanities citizens in this illegal system, well it's the Vatican that lays claim to owning the considered human chattle, cattle, serves, slaves, they are of the energy of lucifer that is why they try to lay claim to your, body, mind and soul that of your eternal divine essense of the immortal interdimensional light being angelic divine energetic consciousness, that you truly be Eternal Spirit Cosmic Consciousness of the Oneness of creation, so the Satanic Vatican of Lucifer is claiming to own which is inside of your biological human avatar body. This is just another level of programming indoctrination and brain washing fron the psychological departments of the demonic cult for obedience for manipulated control by design from there warfare worldwide strategy platform, this is so negative and dark energy of low vibrational energies of these demonic, satanic entites of Lucifer, wicked in intention highly reprehensible vicious immoral with malignancy, cruelty, depravity completely villainous of evil conduct and destructive violence with no conscience, all compassion, kindness dispelled from there beings therefore creating and manifesting in the lowest vibration of the energy of lucifer consciousness, demonic in nature.

22

THE LUCIFERIAN GLOBAL SYSTEM OF GOVERNING CONTROL

So this fallen angel descendants cult of orders that runs the worlds luciferian cults global governing control system, can be perceived in another particular way as the Whore of Babylon as it was claimed and distinctly spoke of in the bible, so this old corporate system is based in the international Maritime Law, so Admirialty Law meaning commonly in the world as Law of The Sea.

This means all of the three city states the city of London, the Pentagon, the Vatican and their and all other corporations in the world, on our planet are governed by Admirialty Law which is Law of the Sea, and they all work together united to keep this Luciferian system in place, expanding its manipulation and control working united in a common goal, to take control of planet earth for themselves to depopulate the planet to a few hundred million enslaved unconsciously remote controlled human chattle, their intention as history shows Genocide on a continuum but now the last big culling is in process, but the light warriors are out there fighting them and taking them down, on behalf of all humanity, then the world citizens will be informed when the sentencing has been carried out, there crimes revealed to the masses many will be shocked in disbelief, then a new start begins for humanity.

So the new quantum grammer system that was set up by Russell Jay Gould has been created to be a present time scenario, system of truth in the moment in the Now Time, also he built in the new quantum periodic table, the new quantum elemental table, which is an extremely clever construct because it took down and crushed the prior old elemental charts of the graphical representation of data in which data is represented by symbols, such as bars in a bar chart, slices in a pie chart, lines in a line chart, also representing tabular numeric data, functions or some kinds of quality structure and that provides different information, therefore a graphical chart representation of data that has multipule meanings.

So when Russell Jay Gould set up this new quantum system and released it he stopped the planets capability of communication, he wiped out the old system and all nations capability to communicate between each other in regards to the control of the shipping lanes of commerce and trade, and so they lost the communication of the movement of cargo commerce, the cause being that they could not create a mathematical code, a mathematical zero point fact to base there sums and differences upon, so the communication between nations came crashing down.

Russel Jay Gould now the Post Master General of the world had to reestablish all commerce and open The United States of America up for business with all the international trading of commerce, which he had to endeavour to fulfilment of the obligation to the United States of America and to the World, he went physically to each location like the universal postal union, the world trade organization, all the big corporations and so registered as the last American standing that had a banking constitution, periodic table, elemental table, his Title Four Flag of a nation, and sovereignty of the world. This allowed him so comfirm that he, his nation is open for trade, commerce, business and so he had to set these key places on planet earth up on the new quantum grammer system of truth, this system prevents all fraud on the planet within the system, as he set there new quantum systems up it disqualified the previous systems that were found to be fraudulent with grammer fraud and so corrupt by the syntax key of the new quantum system.

This is also because he built the new truth quantum construct for communication, now the old systems have crashed he goes to each location to open commerce for The United States off America, and to reestablish setting there new systems of communication correctly and put it online, starting it up with access for them to operate, to be able to track and conduct business, commerce, then you can also perceive that the old corrupt fraudulent system that of maritime law, admiralty law that's belief that souls are lost at sea or dead is seen as the whore of Babalon.

This is in ancient texts the prince of darkness the knave, Lucifer the Devil in his maya of the mind was caused offence supposedly by man, when the devil was in the position at the floor of the throne of God, the devil spoke in anger in a state of rage saying man was already no longer living, deceased, that man was dead.

This was the Devil trying to recreate a reflection of what God had supposedly achieved, manifested, by creating great floods, to destroy man so the devil has done this instead by the archonic system of slavery with the corrupt fraudulent system of birth certificates, that claim this fictional character attached to the birth certificate that is not you as its not living and is an illusion of trickey by the Devils Knavish ways of deceit. It is the energy of Lucifer behind the Vatican, its esoteric dark energy symbolism, the City of London and the Pentagon with its warfare platform, to control, manipulate and deseed humanity and take planet Gaia for themselves.

When Russell Jay Gould had disqualified the old fraudulent corrupt grammer system of all past documents on earth as fraud he had to go to the universal postal union which is a special organization of the corrupt United Nations it is located in Berne, Switzerland, this organization is extremely significant in the world, it was formulated by treaty, as no nation can be recognized as a nation with out being in international admiralty in order to have a forum common to all nations for engaging in commerce and for resolving disputes. Upon his arrival they were told the old system was now dissolved as the old system was of grammer fraud and installing the new system, so going to furnish an equivalent and substitute it with the truth time now grammer system which means fraud cannot take place, as it is the grammer of infinity of truth.

This meant Russell Jay Gould took the position of Universal Post Master in Berne, Switzerland and became Universal Post Master of planet earth, the world, this meant as he took this position he reconstructed anew adjusted and replaced the old perspective of the whore of Babylon to make good to set right with reversal and to rectify, the act of the deceivers of the energy of Lucifer that diverted and deviated the course of humanity, but with this truth version, Russell Jay Gould changed the perspective to The Bride of Christ.

So now you have a system that is correct and true that collapsed the entire world powers on earth with these changes, the new system that is the same as the old system that The United States was using and all the World, but without fraud able to take place of contract grammer fraud as you can't cheat the system with deceit of theft as there are no more loop holes like in the old fraudulent grammer contracts, because of the mathematical certified grammer meaning certified backwards and forwards and then forwards and backwards, so what it means is what it says, and what it says is what it means in the new grammer contracts, so that no one entity or collective of entities that form a company or corporation in the future will not be able to go into a court and twist the meaning of the contract from the past intention when created, so if you had to go into court and argue that the past intention and meaning did not mean what it actually says in the contract, the mathematical quantum grammer does not allow the past or future verbiage or tense of the existance for the manner of words to be expressed to exist therefore the content of the contract is in the Now Time Quantum Grammer, the present always and forever, meaning even in a several hundred years it is still the same meaning in the contract and still stands in that future time in there present time of now.

So in use now is the quantum truth Now Time grammer system that all nations on earth have to use, to commense and conduct commerce.

The Patriot of The Republic of The United States of America Russell Jay Gould basically recreated this new Quantum Grammer construct of form by combining or arranging parts or elements so rebuilt, contrived and devised a new construct in a sentence with the meaning of words used correctly. This put him in danger as it made him powerful enemies.

23

THE REASON BEHIND THE THREE GREAT FLOODS & THE FALLEN ANGELS DESCENDANTS PERSPECTIVE OF GOD

The truth about the three Great floods on our planet Gaia mother earth, Pachamama is that when the the Fallen Angels (not human, its in the words the fallen angels) descended upon the earth to the southern region of Antartica and moved in under ground to an ancient base that the Ancient Builder races created, and combined with

the advanced technologies from their three disabled space fairing craft, after being in a supposed conflict with the Draco race and kicked of the moon, there craft were damaged and unable to leave this solar system, and so set up base in this location on earth. (They the fallen angels were on the moon for an approximate one hundred and twenty thousand years, before that their ancestors lived on the super earth Merbec that was destroyed, (and is now the asteroid belt) by there evil plans to utilise the advanced technology field that protected the 52 solar systems in our star cluster from Genetic Farmer races, this technology was built and left in place by the ancient builder races so stop genetic farming of races, species in this star cluster.)
When they arrived on earth and settled they the fallen angels proceeded to start messing with humanity and our genetics, this was not taken kindly by the fortyish races conducting twenty two genetic manipulations on humanity, for humanity to raise our consciousness and to be able

to access our DNA informational pool in which there is the schematic blueprint instructions to grow your eternal light body, passing the karmic cycles of life and death, being fully embodied but having access to all dimensions of the hyper-dimensional matrix of creation by travelling in our light bodies enveloped in a sixty foot field of light, no space craft needed or by instant teleportation once you comprehend past wave form energy to powdered light form understanding of energy.

So the forty races caused The Great Floods times three to wipe out the Fallen Angels to stop the evil intent of humanities genetic manipulation, it worked at that time they were flooded out of there bases losing there technologies and many died but they say around a couple of thousand survived, there descendants we know now who are now the Disgraced Fallen Angel two Royal Israelite bloodlines The House of Saud and the British German European Royals, there intention to take planet Gaia for themselves and keep a small few hundred million human slaves for there needs and to genocide the rest of humanity.

Why well from there perspective God wiped out most of there race there ancestors so their vendetta is to mirror the same and wipe most of humanity out going against creation, anti life in there manifested intention, this is why they do what they do, they conduct dark negative magic in ancient blood ceremonies and human sacrifice to summon up energy entities that have no avatars, biological bodies from the $4^{th}/5^{th}$ dimensions, they are known in ancient texts as The Jinn The Archons, they are Demons and Devils with the vibration and energy of Lucifer the energy of Satan and the descendants give them clone bodies or use body hoping practices and technologies to place there soul into another body after removing the consciousness of the original occupant, but hold no hate or fear as when you start to access God Consciousnes you perceive they are us for we are all one in creation, expressing dark and light in this duality reality. This is why they hate humanity it's a vendetta against the creator for the reaction of their anscestors actions to genetically manipulate humanity and doing so with no authority to do so causing there races destruction and dimise of there terminally mentally ill ancestors, for blood sacrifice, human sacrifice, and child blood consumption is forbidden from the immortal and mortal perception.

24

THE ROYAL FALLEN ANGEL CULT LOSE THEIR LEGAL POWERS

The royal fallen angel cult lose all there legal powers and sovereignty powers of The United States and Great Britan and all Great Britain reigns over, then they want revenge so they illegally kidnap Russell Jay Gould they rough him up torture and beat him to try to make him relinquish the United Sates Title Four Flag, but to no avail with no success as this patriot was standing in his power, defient to these British enemy agents, War Criminal of the Blood Sacrifice cult.

The Criminal Royal Cult and its minions procceded to take him to court because Russell Jay Gould started to court marshel Dick Cheney, George W Bush, and around Five Hundred Admirals and Generals that were traitors of The United States, this is because they carried on the illegal fraud of the old system, and did not immediately changing over to the new quantum system of truth, and the new government not being implemented from the top of government to the bottom to the civil level, this means the contracts at state and civil levels then would be operating on the new legal quantum construct system of truth, this was because Russell Jay Gould the New sovereign of The United States and Great Britan wanted to immediately stop the corruption of fraud, the laundering of money used to move illegal gun running, drug trafficking, human trafficking of women and children, to stop pedophile money laundering, and stop illegal trading of gold.

The new quantum construct system would show were the money was going, this meant you could not borrow from peter to pay paul, so from one government fund to another this stopped the corruption in house in government funds, accounts, another example is taking money from colleges to pay for highway maintence, but in the cult criminal case to buy guns, drugs, human traffick or finance terrorists, so the old corrupt borrowing system would collapse, this is why Russell Jay Gould insisted this correction was made immediately, this is why he court marshelled the Admirals and Generals and Cult criminal members.

25

THE ILLEGAL APPOINTMENT OF THE ROYAL BLOOD CULT CRIMINAL GEORGE W BUSH TO PRESIDENT OF THE UNITED STATES OF AMERICA WHO WAS CRIMINALLY UNELECTED

The War Criminal George W Bush was not elected he was appointed as the world knows the election was corrupted and rigged so it was fraudulent, as many world citizens already know the crime family of the Clintons, the Obamas

Barack a muslim brotherhood member (which if you do not recognize that Islam is a political militant organization hiding behind a religion falsely that this the fallen angel House of Saud created to use for its bidding) and his gay lover from college Micheal LaVon Robinson now a transgender called Michelle Obama, and George W Bush were put in there positions by the disgraced fallen angels descendants royal Israelite Blood Cult of Sacrifice also known as the the New World Order, the Shadow Government, the Globalists, the Deep State, the group of thirteen bloodlines with there worldwide control system of infiltration in world governments and corporations, there machine of banking, surveillance, intelligence, there organizations The World Health Organization, the CDC, The United Nations, the Pentagon, the Vatican, the City of London, there aim to imprison all of the whole worlds citizens of the earths surface human population, so to take by FORCE HUMANITY to control and ensnare by trickery, manipulation the entire human race by the illegal fraudulent birth certificate slavery system.

At that time War Criminal George W Bush got in to power fraudulently and Russell Jay Gould had rushed and moved so fast in his setting up of the new quantum system and as Postal Master General and all the required legal procedures, he had had a moment of inattention which was imperative and had not informed the military with particular information at this particular step in his planned procedure, at this stage of his Patriotic Plan to save his beloved Republic of The United States of America, which was he did not inform the NCO Chain of Command control centre, and let them know his plan of this particular strategy he was using at this stage of his endeavour, to inform them the military of the progress of the Bancrupty of the United States and that they were to be surrendered to the Great Britan and there flag to be raised and The Republic of The United States of

America to be Surrendered, meaning the United States of America citizens would be prisoner slaves so chattle, then the invasion would first deceptively go after your only means of defense, that's your weapons, then citizens would be sent to the Federal Emergency Management Agency prison camps that are in place with millions of plastic coffins spread out in states all over the United States today, the Treasonous traitors Obama was setting it up and if Hillary Clinton got into office in 2016 and exerted her War Criminal plans it was the end of freedom for United States of america citizens and the end of The Republic of The United States of America and world domination.

26

THE CULTS LANGUAGE OF WORDS THE TRICKERY OF THE TONGUE OF THERE SATANIC DOUBLE SPEAK

One example to start is (servicing the target) actually meaning (for bombing), or other euphemisms like (downsizing or layoffs) there language that deliberately obscures, distorts, disguises and reverses the meanings of words, this is primarily meant to make the truth sound more palatable, so there language that can be understood in more than one way and that is used to trick and deceive people, the United States citizens and world citizens, it's a language which pretends to communicate but dosen't it's a language which makes the Bad seem Good, the Negative seem Postitive, the Unpleasant seem Unattractive or least Tolerable, it's a language that Avoids Shifts or Denies Responsibility, so it's a language which is at variance with its real or purported meaning, hiding the Truth by Deception, to further there Satanic Luciferian Agenda.

When looking into there language infrastructure that they have set up when you research and go back in time and examine methodically by sperating into parts and studying their interrelations, you start to perceive what they actually really mean the great example is the famous speech made by President George Bush Seniors double speak of trickery an example is (Quote - We have before us the opportunity to forge for ourselves and for our future generations a New World Order, a world were the rule of law, not the law of the jungle, governs the conduct of nations, or Quote - A world were the strong respect the rights of the weak). What this actually means is when refers to the weak it means the one percent the thirteen bloodlines the new world satanic order, this is because humanities worldwide citizens are the ninty nine percent of the planets population, so they are the weak, we the people are the strong but only if UNITED AS ONE WORLD CONNECTED UNIFED, to connect our co-creative consciousness to dispel them from the existance of planet Gaia our Mother Earth Pachamama, we humanity the Eternal Light beings manifesting into these human avatars for a three dimensional experience of expression of the Divine, with the energy of the Creator of the Oneness of the whole collective Consciousness of The Brahaman, The Whole, The Creation, to then wake up to our true multidimensional reality of the universe, cosmos the hyper-dimensional matrix and to realise we are are eternal immortal divine angelic light being goddesses and gods caretakers of stars systems, caretakers so the stewards of all sentient life in the multiverses in the eternal realms of the Kingdom of Light outside of time and space, and inside time and space in the multiverses, we world citizens do not want this satanic demonic blood cult world order, we chose nature, spirit, the divine, we choose life, with intentions of love light compassion understanding, creating magic wonder and beauty for all races and cultures to express there divine creative energy as they choose with support and empathy.

The fallen angel descendants the royal Israelite Davidic Goldsmith Zionest Satanic Demonic bloodlines have already told the world of there plans they don't hide them, its in ancient scriptures and in plain site in movies, tv shows, music industry sound and visual, as they try to subvert humanity to depravity, slavery and genocide, they have told us of there intended satanic lucifarian manifested agendas.

So what did War Criminal George W Bush Senior mean when he said (Quote- To protect the weak from the strong, to have freedom and peace) he was talking about having the freedom for the cult to stop the ninty nine percent of humanity from stopping there satanic agenda to stop there lucifarian take over of the world, by stopping them making illegal laws freely at there will in peace, so that humanity the ninty nine percent cannot stop them from there satanic take over of the world agenda and to try to stop humanity stopping, so preventing the Genocide of Humanity.

This cults language their actions and intentions are vicious and villainous completely wicked and extremely highly reprehensible and offensive in charcter, in there conduct and in there evil nature they are morally corrupted with moral depravity which can cannote malignancy with cruelty and with intented destructive violence they are vile in there negative manifested nature.

When the language is studied you realize that they the cult members are not communicating or talking to the United States citizens or the worlds people its actually communicating with its own fallen angel Royal Israelite cult members of the thirteen satanic bloodlines, they are communicating with there higher up command of chain in the cult.

27

THE MATHEMATICAL GRAMMER FACT CONSTRUCT & THE MILITARY NOT BEING INFORMED & NEW GOVERNMENT TO BE ESTABLISHED PART 1

So the Pariot of The Republic of The United States of America Russell Jay Gould had ceased power from the cult legally and now world Postal Master General and has Sovereignty over The United States of America and Great

Britan, remember this happened on 2nd november 1999, this meant the entire law of the sea, the maritime law, the admiralty law system had collapsed because Russell Jay Gould created an entire new system on Now Time Quantum Grammer Construct an infinity of truth system, always meaning when read (contracts) in the now time the meaning the same in the present of the future moment of now always and forever, this also meant all the codes, statues, and laws in relation to the illegal fraudulent law of the sea, so admiralty law were now in the quantum mathematical grammer construct fact, this invalidated, ruled out and prohibited the old system construct of fraud.

Now the new Sovereignty of the United States of America and of Great Britan the new World Postal Master General the new Commander General Russell Jay Gould stopped the satanic luciferian new world orders tyranical take over of the world.

At that time the thirteen bloodlines of the cult because of the strategic moves Russell JayGould had played in defeating them at there own evil game of trickery and deception, but he put all of his plays in the plan together so swiftly that he only informed the upper levels of military command the non commissioned officers chain of command that he had taken control and command of the United States of America but his miss step of over seeing to inform the upper levels of military, this meant they were not informed to rally behind him and support him and protect him, with gratitude for salvaging The Republic of The United States of America their nation and now their new Commander and Chief, and saving the entire enslavement of the planet and that of humanity.

Russell Jay Gould had succeded in his plans halting the new world orders royal Israelite agendas instantly, the only thing that prevented this was not having the militaries support as he moved so swiftly he didn't inform all the rest of the military so this left him vunerable, the cult criminals in power by fraud like George W Bush Junior pushed him, booted him to the curb and to the side and they set up the Federal Reserve so that the Criminal Rothschild banker family could move into United States Territory and they Illegally and Crimminally took over as Post Master General at the Post Office of Washington District of Columbia and place a new illegal criminal Post Master General in his position, this evidence of this is all recorded in the Congressional Record and you can find this information in the 1999 government reclamation act. As the end of the final bankruptcy of the United States was now Null and Void through the Patriot Russell Jay Goulds Valient efforts this meant a new government needed to formed and structured with elected nominees by the United States citizens.

27

THE MATHEMATICAL GRAMMER FACT CONSTRUCT & THE MILITARY NOT BEING INFORMED & NEW GOVERNMENT TO BE ESTABLISHED PART 2

So this War Criminal Royal Cult and its orders and the Masonic Lodges The Knights of Columbus, The Knights of Saint Thomas, The Knights of Malta, The Knights of Lazarus, The Knights Templar, The Knights Hospitaller the

Knights of Saint John the Teutonic Knights and the Assasins of the Jesuit Order the Rothschilds bloodline that are at the top of this pyramid of and as Jesuit agents operating under a Kahzarian Jewish cover who formed the Illuminati back in 1776, so effectively this throws the onus of this conspiracy on the Darl Kahzarian Jews and the other Jesuits the Morgans and Rockerfellers they all do the bidding of the Jesuit Order and they are doing everything in there power to destroy the constitutional liberty in The United States of America and of the entire world. These bloodlines were furious extremely angry there two hundred year plan was dismantled by one Patriot of The Republic of The United States of America the one and only Legend Russell Jay Gould, this is because he was independent and did not have the ideology or beliefs of the cult orders the masonic lodges, therefore not controllable as he is a citizen of The Republic of The United States of America he is an American citizen in there eyes seen as chattle a slave, so therefore an enemy of the cult bloodlines orders and agendas.

So they have this Intelligent American Civillian Patriot that had the mental acute judgment and rationality to workout and understand and to solve the crisis of The Republic of The United States of America being taken over and surrendered to and by these War Criminal Royal Cult bloodlines and there orders and masonic lodge members that are working for the English Crown meaning the Queen of England therefore working on behalf of Great Britan.
This meant the Patriot Russell Jay Gould could not be blackmailed as this is the standard control practice of the royal cult, and he was not in any compromised position to be blackmailed, the cult of child sacrifice and pedeophilia could not set him up with illegal or criminal business practices or for child crimes or for extortion, as he is clean and his action of good intention saved his beloved Republic of The United States of

America and at the same time he created set up and installed a new worldwide now time quantum matimatical grammer construct with its new Periodic table of elements, what an absolute legend Russell Jay Gould is, a true Republican Patriot.

This is why they the criminal cult under no circumstances do they want or are willing to allow him to take over and be in control, to have full tactical command and control as he has placed and positioned himself to be, because they could not blackmail him to control him, so he will not do there evil intended bidding for there dark lucifaian agenda.

This patriot was operating under his own set of rules and the direction of his own moral compass and would hold fast, stick to and adhere to the new quantum system of truth. The cult knows this patriot is not prepared to and will not play by there fraudulent corrupt illegal rules, regulations, statues, laws that are the make up of the cults entire criminal structure of which is fraudulent by way of Grammer Fraud.

28

AFTER TWELVE YEARS OF CONTINUED ILLEGAL CONTROL OF THE UNITED STATES BY THE CULT CRIMINALS

After twelve years the true real sovereignty of The United States of America Russell Jay Gould had had enough of the continuation of the criminal organization of the Royal British enemy Agents that were still occupying the top levels of the American government and the military, that had refused to correct the corrupt system and go in the direction of the truth Now Time quantum system, and that this factual system had not be recognized and implemented immediately, and to recognize the truth and facts of what acheviments actually manifested and were created and to what events actually took place at that time, in the world in relation to the United States of America final bankruptcy, that a Patriot of The Republic of The United States of America had seized the Title Four Flag, and that Russell Jay Gould had logged in at the United Nations, and at that point Russell Jay Gould was declared a sovereignty and that he had taken control and command of the Post Office of Washington District of Columbia, and that he took the position of tactical command and control of The United States of America and all of the powers of war.

When this great Patriot realized the cult criminal members were ingoring him he set up the new worldwide quantum construct went around the world and set up his government system of Now Time grammer truth and as he set up in each nation he would take down the old fraudulent system as he set up the new true correct Now Time quantum grammer system.

Also the American citizens were not told the truth of the hugely enormously significant and major event that had taken place and occurred on 2 november 1999 and events there after, the citizens were not told of the need to set up ane elect a new president and his roll the parameters of his position the limit of that what he may need to control aspects of governance and that would be the administrator of the governance of finances to be distributed equally and logically for the benefit of all citizens of The United States of America and for defense and joint world projects for the benefit of all humanity, also to setup a new senate, a new congress, a new banking constitution, because when you perceive it as the system for the United States did not come to forecloser or an end but the new quantum system had to be put in place and recognized and implemented in its full capacity.

Then another big move and play by the Patriot was after this continued fraudulent system still in business twelve years later after the 1999 collapse of the third bankruptcy of the United States, these criminals that had put in and set up the illegal Federal Reserve by the criminal bankers, and even up to now today carried on as the criminals they are illegally for the last twenty years, all working with and together, are these criminal royal british cult agents with George W bush Junior being one of the many main culprets.
So Russell Jay Gould and David Wynn Miller decided to on the twenty first of December 2012 to open up The Benjamin Franklin Post Office in Philadelphia

Pennsylvania, but understand that the Washington District of Columbia its under law of the sea, maritime law so Admiralty law because this was the jurisdiction of the King of England or Queen of England in todays times this is the standard operating system of the crowns warfare platform and how they run Great Britan, and they consider the british public chattle assumed to be cargo a vessel, missing at sea or dead, this is understood to be under the jurisdiction of the sea, so jurisdiction of Admiralty law.

Then we come to law of the land the civil jurisdiction which is in Philadelphia, Pennsylvania, were the Patriots Russell Jay Gould and David Wynn Miller opened up the Benjamin Franklin Post Office, this post office had been closed since the start of the American Revolution and could not reopened as it could not contract for commerce because of the bankruptcy of The United States of America and the debt of one point six million francs that was owed to the nation of France. So this why the King of England had to open there post office in Washington District of Columbia at the time if the king did not do this France or spain sovereignty would of come in and opened there own post office.

29

THE OPENING UP OF THE BENJAMIN FRANKLIN POST OFFICE IN PHILADELPHIA PENNSYLVANIA IN THE JURISDICTION OF LAW OF THE LAND

When Russell Jay Gould opened this post office to commerce he actually had opened the entire system back up at the original location and planted, so posted the Title Four United States of America

Flag at this position now occupied by this Sovereignty Pariot Russell Jay Gould, this meant because he did this and because the illegal birth certificate system had ended, he could now present all citizens with the claim of LIFE, so the citizens are no longer considered missing lost at sea or dead, so that meant he was shipping citizens out of the land of the dead and so bringing citizens onto the land, and under civil jurisdiction to Law of The Land, where your BLOOD testifies as proof of Life, this means by doing so Russell Jay Gould reconstituted the whole United States of American Government, in the correct procedure under the right true Title Four United States Flag, using the truth time now grammer quantum communication system, this then allowed this Patriot to reestablish his systems of global governance around the world, so all nations and peoples could conduct commerce with out fraud, this means in The United States and in Great Britan the old illegal rules, statues, laws do not have any validility and do not stand up in court from the old fraudulent system and have all been DISQUALIFIED.

30

THE YEAR 2017

The Patriot and Post Office Master General and Commander and Chief of the United States of America Russell Jay Gould returns to Washington District of Columbria and goes to the Federal Reserve to confront the infiltrated War Criminals of the Royal British Cult, because the building was supposed to have vacated, so deprived of an incumbent or occupant and should of relinquished possession of the property and left the area totally devoid of contents, as the New Post office Master General of the United States and of The world, his court judgment has cancelled and rendered there occupancy null and void and they the criminals were evicted by order of the now correct quantum grammer system of now time truth construct court system judgment, and were supposed to have vacated the entire continent of The United States of America, as the end of the final third bankruptcy has occurred and been finalized and legally complete due to grammer fraud and corruption.

This meant that the internal revenue service that had been operating and was the collection agency for the DEAD supposed chattle citizens of the United States of America, had to be removed from the nation, so the federal reserve was supposed to have ended seventeen years earlier but had continued operating illegally in a fraudulent fashion by the criminal Rothschild Bankers that did not leave and so the Patriot the Commander and Chief Russell Jay Gould arrives at the Post Office of Washington District of Columbia and informs the illegal illegitimate British Royal Blood Cult Agents, this building is not allowed to be docked on my land, so therefore I as commander and chief I am imposing a fine against you the board of governers of the Federal Reserve for having this vessel/building docked on his land as sovereignty of The United States the commander and chief and Post Master General, the fine was massive it was huge to a total of seventeen million tons of gold. This gold asset now belonging to The Republic of the United States of America, the Commander and Chief Russell Jay Gould wishes to use to supplementary, so to aid in the reestablishment, so to reestablish The United States of Americas Government by using and allowing to have the new quantum system of Now Time grammer of truth backed up by gold reserves, this then places values on his stock market platform, his banking system, so international commerce could take place in the correct and proper manner.

His wishes were to help aid President Donald John Trump and General James Mattis the secretary of defense who was in the United States cabinet under President Donald John Trump and aid the entire United States military and the citizens of the nation to rebuild a new monetary system and get The United States Of America back in business for trading, shipping and commerce. Its been said Russell Jay Gould tried to inform President Donald John Trump of his efforts and accumplishments and that of his procedures and plans, and this patriots wishes were to legitimise President trumps authority and back his plans for The United States of America, he wanted to stand with the president and help clean out the enemy criminal infiltrators of the british monarchs royal coven cult criminal agents. This is because earlier in the previous times of 1999 the Patriot Russell Jay Gould had tried to clean house with the United States Government but had been thwarted at every attempt from enemies within house, so within government in the higher levels of power, he tried to dismantle there illegal strangle hold of his beloved Republic, but had trouble putting these plans in effect he could not do it because of his mishap of not informing the military back in 1999, this is why the british invading enemies that had infiltrated the nations government had booted him aside and carried on there illegal occupation of the Republic of The United States of America, this the same shadow government, deep state, cabal, the royal fallen angel illuminati blood sacrifice satanic, demonic Israelite cult, that President Donald John Trump in fighting to remove from office and remove from power from within The United States Government and Military, he may of left office of the United States Corporation, but its believed Donald John Trump is still the President of The Republic of The United States of America and at this time has left the United States Military in charge to remove any enemy conspiritors from office and from power in the military, intelligence agencies, law enforcement those enemies of the fallen angel british cult and enemies from China and any other nations. Its believed that the military has staged the Joe Biden inauguration to stop the criminal democrats organizations and funded groups of Antifa, communist groups, fascist groups and foreign enemy agents from burning down cities as they had cited to do so publicly by these groups words and actions, if Joe Biden did not get into office. So it appears that this keeps United States cities safer and its citizens, while the military arrests members of this criminal satanic cult, and government members, while simultaneously conducting military operation underground to cease control of the DEEP UNDERGROUND BASES known as DUMBS and then to conduct operations deeper into the earths catacombs of chambers and tunnels and in the maze of the earths labyrinths of passage ways and caves to remove these satanic demonic traitors of The United States of America and that of the Worlds Citizens for the War Crimes of Genocide of Humanity, to be put to death in military tribunals.

31

THE BIGGEST NATIONAL SECURITY THREAT OF THE REPUBLIC OF THE UNITED STATES OF AMERICA & THE WHOLE WORLD & ITS CONNECTION TO THE 2007 MORTGAGE COLLAPSE & THE FALL OF THE DISGRACED 13 ROYAL BLOODLINES

This secret has been kept for a long time and is now being revealed to The United

States Citizens and Citizens of the World as the biggest national security threat of The Republic of The United States of America and the biggest threat to all nations on Mother Earth, a threat to all cultures and races on planet Gaia, a Satanic, Demonic Lucifarian threat to HUMANITY and all sentient LIFE on this planet Gaia our Mother Earth, Pachamama.

So the connection to the collapse of the United States morgage market is that all this secret hidden information about the third bankruptcy of The United States of America and the installation of the new Now Time grammer quantum system of construct and the evidence is all there in the Presidential documented papers and in the Congressional documented papers its all recorded, the good souls in the American Military and its special forces have spoken and stepped in line to defeat these enemies of Evil energies of Darkness that have manifested into human avatars or jumped into human clones to attempt a take over of the Planet

Gaia and Humanity for the cause and agenda of the negative Maya Energy of Lucifer.

And with the collapse of the mortgage crisis the truth came out about the fall and lose of power and control as Sovereignty of The United Kingdom and the intended take over of The United States of America by the English Crown the English Monarch.

So Queen Elizabeth the Second has no power or Legitamacy in the World today. The Grotesque repulsive Queen her disgusting Family of child torturers, child murderers are the fallen and disgraced Fallen Angel descendants the Goldsmith Davidic Israelite Jewish Zionist Satanic Demonic Bloodlines of the Orders of a Blood Cult of child sacrifice and pedophilia, for they are NOT HUMAN they are Draco Reptilian in nature and with the energy of Lucifer, they are demonic in nature, its in the title remember THE FALLEN ANGELS meaning NOT HUMAN, a negative draco reptilian in nature feeds of loosh energy that is generated by organic life in varying degrees of purity, the clearest and most potent coming from Humans- engendered by Human activity which tigers emotion, the highest of such emotion coming from humans feeling threatened, harmed or being tortured then killed the results in the traumatizing pain and suffering that is experienced and recorded in the biological avatar body, mind and in the consciousness of the soul the eternal spirit that inhabits the human biological avatar, this trauma and pain is also recorded in the body consciousness of our Mother Earth itself. The worst crimes these Draco reptilians and Royal half breeds commit is the feeding of human blood after torture has occurred creating huge amounts of adrenaline, this blood enriched with adrenaline is called Adrenochrome and it is the royal family and Satanic Cult members drug of choice for its anti aging properties, DEVILS and DEMONS they truly be, of the energy of of The JINN The ARCHONS which are the Devils and Demons which is the energy of Lucifer. One must keep in mind not all Draco or reptilians are negative or evil one must keep that understanding in there perspective.

32

THE TRUTH OF UNITED NATION FLAG SYSTEM

The legitimate flags of nations do not have a yellow fringe on the circumference of the flag, all flags around the world that are registered with the corrupt criminal organization of the United Nations, all flags registered in there copyright and pattern do not have a yellow fringe on them, this yellow fringe was further joined to the circumference of

The United States Title Four Flag at a later date, because everything/everyone has been apprehended captured and conquered or in the process of being conquered and seized and over run by illegitimate criminals intend on world domination.

So because everything/everyone has been apprehended by the illegal (because law of the sea is being used in place of the law of the land, meaning it is null and void) Maritime Law, Admiralty Law, the Law of the Sea, so captured by the jurisdiction of the Admiralty Law this means the United States citizens and world citizens have been seized in a shipping war. The yellow fringes intention insinuates and symbolizes that The Title Four Flag has been seized so captured by this shipping war, by this shipping warfare platform used to enslave humanity and take full dominant control of planet earth, all its resources including humanity. This shipping warfare platform is based in the international Maritime, Admiralty Law, Law of the Sea, this means the yellow fringed flag does not belong to any nation on earth, it does not have a nation as its jurisdiction over the sea and the sea is not a nation, the sea is not legally registered as a nation with the corrupt criminal organization of the United Nation.

This means when the Patriot of The Republic of The United States of America Russell Jay Gould commandeered The Title Four Flag Of The United States of America from the Pentagon with there expressed blessing, understanding The United States of America was about to be surrendered, he removed the yellow fringe from the circumference of The Title Four Flag, he did this because in the United States in army regulations it states that this is a violation, a desecration, a defilement of the flag so it was immediately removed to symbolize that he had smashed and by doing so completely destroyed the illegal Fraudulent international Maritime Law, Admiralty Law, Law of the Sea, being used illegally and criminally as Law of the Land.

So when this Patriot of The Republic of The United States of America Russell Jay Gould removed the yellow fringe from the Title Four Flag he had seized the Law of the Sea, so Admiralty Law, under which is the illegal criminal illegal Corporation Law that's governed by Statue Law meaning Law of Fraudulent Contracts and made it Null and Void, this meant he had released the citizens the people from the shipping warfare platform by shipping them back to the land of the Living under Jurisdiction of Law of the Land under Universal Common Law.

33

CONCLUSION OF THESE HISTORIC CHANGES

The new Now Time Quantum mathematical grammer construct system of truth that is unable to allow fraud in any capacity this will rebalance the world to earth citizens it will also after the wealth is confliscated from the fallen thirteen bloodlines and dispersed between world nations to rebuild there nations from the cities to the villages and wealth distributed to the citizens of humanity, this will change fundamentally the lives of earths citizens also to be released are hidden advanced technologies that will be distributed to the worlds citizens of medical technologies, also in time free zero point energy technologies, anti-gravity technologies, communication technologies, manifesting replication technologies creating what you need instantly at a few touches of a button. Russell Jay Goulds new quantum system of now Time mathematical grammer construct was declared genius by the department of energy, it is so important that the entire world and the United States embraces this new quantum system as this system has its own periodic table elemental chart it is genius and the united states and the world must immediately espouse meaning to take the opinion of the policies and practices and accept and implement this quantum system, if not then the Forces of the Darkness of Evil will commender this system spelling extreme imminent danger, an immediate threat to the planet Gaia our Mother Earth, Pachamama a living conscious being, and an absolute immediate threat to all of humanity as a whole civilization and all sentient life on the earth.

As we come to understand this quantum mathematical grammer construct of Now Time that is used to form contracts on this planet Gaia, but if the good do not use it the negative forces will and this would be fatal as they would start creating contracts and subject the world citizens and the United States to there negative intentioned will in connection to this quantum construct, as they will squash, force, and destroy World citizens and citizens of the United States of America, they will make laws that are set in stone solid never changeable, regulations that are ironclad, the only thing stopping them is the fact that the Syntax key stamp of legitimacy must be on any contract also with Russell Jay Goulds signature and his thumb print on each and every document, then if not on the documents they are considered null and void as they are not substantiated as evidence and proof of truth, in relation to the contract with the substantiated excutive authority that is necessary and must be provided as required to legitamise these type of legal contract documents, if not then the documents are not legal and are considered fraudulent. They cannot get around the periodic table and elemental chart of the new quantum construct stopping them is the mathematical construct of grammer as its in Now time, so what it says it means now and forever, so it's a fact in the present or in the future Now time years from now, its just a factual system of truth with the loop of infinity symbol as varication.

Remember this new quantum grammer system has removed all fraud from the constructs of grammer, so the enemies of humanity the two non-human fallen royal bloodlines with the thirteen families the seven orders there masonic lodges, the minions of satanic and demonic forces of the negative Draco reptilian energies of The JINN The ARCHONS with the Evil Darkness energy of Lucifer, they do not have the ability to move forward from this new quantum system in the characteristic or customary mode of acting with affectiveness or with the presence of the correct demeanor, tone and manner, that would allow them the dark forces to disqualify this new quantum grammer type of platform. Its impossible they can not beat or cheat this system of truth in Now Time grammer, so the United States and the world must unite with the new system embrace it or the enemies of humanity the dark negative forces will take it and use it against the world citizens to enslave but a few of humanity and genocide the rest of the whole of humanity, ALL LIFE ON EARTH IS IN DANGER OF BEING enslaved or Extinct if these FALLEN ANGEL descendants the ROYAL GOLDSMITH DAVIDIC ZIONIST SATANIC DEMONIC BLOOD CULT of Sacrifice and the House of Saud bloodlines must be removed from the surface of the earth, from the underground of the earth, from this planet and from existance they must be exterminated, so they there souls can pay there debts in karma and after be reborn a healthy productive member of the cosmic societies, with the up liftment of others and for the benefit of the oneness of creation for them to be in service of spirit of the divine oneness of creation, for we are all one at the end of the day, connected united in a unified field of eternal conscious light energy, namaste Amen blessings to all sentient life in The Brahaman, The Whole, The Creation.

34

UNDERSTANDING THE NEW QUANTUM FINANCIAL BANKING SYSTEM

Did you know that the President Donald John Trump Adminstration has committed to the new mathematical grammer Quantum Financial System to release its amazingly incredible speed and potential for The United States of America and that of the worlds economic growth, and for technological advancement and for national security purposes. To coordinate a national research effort encompassing Federal agencies, the academic community, and industrial leaders already underway, The White House National Quantum Coordination Office has released A Strategic Vision for America's Quantum Financial System Networks, this was released in February in the year 2020.

The New Quantum Financial System has the support and backing so the commitment of the biggest financial institutions in the world these are the United States Treasury, and the Heritage Fund, also ninty seven percent of the world banks.

The Quantum financial System (QFS) provides a pristine clean integrity in the movement of funds from Central Banking sources to destination accounts.

The (QFS) will cover the new global network for the transfer of asset backed

funds and will replace the United States Centrally Controlled Swift System.
The main benefits and its key point of (QFS) is that this system protects all parties from fraudulent corruption, usury and manipulation from within the banking system and ensure banks are monitored and protected with to the agreed upon contract of the transfer fund process.

The Cross Border Inter-bank Payment System (CIPS) this includes and consists of the Quantum Financial System (QFS), also Cross Border Inter-bank Payment System (CIPS), also Artifical Intelligence (AI), also Virtual Private Network (VPN), also QFS 3D Smart Phone, also included is Asset-Backed Digital Currencies.

The Quantum Financial System (QFS) is completely independant from the existing centralized systems and makes all others transfer systems absolete due to its advanced capabilities.

The Quantum Financial System (QFS) is Definitively Not a Crypto-currency but instead it is asset-backed digital currency. The Quantum Financial System (QFS) reigns supreme in the photonics technology at three point five trillion frames per second, it replaces obsolete IP dynamic routing with true physical GPS authentication between sender and receiver routing while upholding one hundred percent financial security and transparency of all currency holders. Protocals will be instituted with (QFS) so that artificial intelligence will control the transfers and independently be allowed to control the global financial network unless the highest levels of approval is given. Artificial intelligence (AI) will handle (instant settlements in real Now TIME, with out delays.

Artificial intelligence (AI) assigns a unique digital number fiat (so then can sanction and give authorization) to every Dollor, Euro, Yen in every bank account all over the world, digital numbers are monitored in real time, the physical GPS location between sender and receiver will be set up to provide unhackable security when it was ledgered with regard to who sent it, and what account received it. Sovereign Currency of The United States of America is the USN.

The location of the Headquarters of the Quantum Financial System is SWITCH Las Vegas.

GOLD-SILVER-MAGNET the GSM RESERVES - The CIPS and structure backing our coins.

Relating to Honest Weights & Measures - Digital Currency a conversion in the future from a fiat crypto currency into a gold backed based 111 (3), IV (4) & V (5) complaint coin.
The coins themselves and the virtual coins will have barcodes (ownership) and GPS (location) tracking devices.

Asset Chain Collection (ACC) is a Distributed General Ledger, it is a tool of the (AI) Asset digitalization it organizes data in terms of blocks that are legged in combination and encrypted for full GPS security. All data transactions exist in history and cannot be altered or deleted, this creates a clean prestine integrity of all transactions.

Blockchain is a Distributed Ledger Technology (DLT), DLT is Blockchain's parent, every Blockchain node is provided its own ledger copy and all instant transactions are encrypted before being added to the ledger.

Blockchain does not require a central authority, it is completely decentralized as DLT and organizes data in terms of blocks that are linked and encrypted for full GPS security.

All data transactions exist in history and cannot be altered or deleted so then creating pristine integrity of all transactions.

Blockchain the structured blocks of data in specific block sequences, Distributed Ledger Technology Databased spread across different nodes with no specific sequence. A unique sequence is that it is distinguishing feature in Blockchain.

Cross-border Inter-bank Payment System (CIPS), Quantum Financial System (QFS), Blockchain is a subset of distributed ledgers, Blockchain takes the Distributed Ledger Technology (DLT) to the next level instantiation to represent by concrete or tangible digital values and enter interoperability.

DLT is the parent to Blochchain Technology and is the means to Eliminate Bank Oversight, creating Transparency and Speed of Transactions.

This means NO DATA can be Compromised, Blockchain is different from DLT in terms of architecture but similar in terms of concept DLT solves issues in the financial realm, Blockhchain is part of the crypto Currency world.

35

HOW TO MANAGE NEW FUNDS ASSET BACKED IN QUANTUM FINANCIAL SYSTEM (QFS)

How do you move and use these funds in the QFS, all bank screens are now dark! In the new system you will receive any notification from AI that you are expected to asset backed funds are available to ledger to the designated account you have previously annotated. You will then have to follow the prompts requiring your old access code password.

Patent P verses NP Problem Space, Building an artificial intellingence (AI) confronts a challenging problem called the P verses NP question. The AI question is whether every problem whose solution can be quickly verified by a computer can also be quickly solved by a computer, some problems can be solved quickly by P. Other problems that cannot be solved quickly but if shown the answer can be verified quickly by NP. P is shorthand for solved in polynomical Time (polynomical ...P).

Solving the Problem the planned fifty six Data Centres units in the United States of America and territories and the planned one hundred and ninty two Data Center units planned globally will increase the overall speed, power and the efficiency of our QFS in a parallel processing environment – The Ultimate QFS Cloud System.
Once entered you will be prompted by AI to create a New Security ID, Once that occurs your old bank account will be

debited of Fiat funds and then credited with asset backed funds One-to-One. You will be prompted to the next window at which point your existing funds show as asset backed as well as the ledger balance of asset backed funds anticipated. There is no co-mingling, The system is totally secure and your accounts are Totally Under your Control, as a process of RETURN to SOVEREIGNTY, You must initiate the ledger, a Photon transaction occurs from sender account to recipient account through physical GPS authentication No other person can access the accounts. Banks are no longer required they are obsolete.

Real Time Data, CIPS provides a real time data feed for all applications attached to it, this means your clients will receive live data directly to desktops, web and other mobile clients all at once.

You have the SOVEREIGNTY of your funds, since all are phonic and digital, all funds are GPS trackable forever, banks are no longer in control, therefore there are no more Deposits, they are noe Posits because deposit means separation from the person and their funds.

In the new financial world the person has No footprint in the QFS, this is ground breaking historical security in the truest sense, in the Now Time Quantum Mathematical Grammer System of Truth.

Explanatory statistical supplementary material texts -
A - Quantum Financial System QFS ends all corruption that could currently exist with regard to the Corrupt Central Banking System.
B – The QFS will cover the new global network for the transfer of asset backed funds, it replaces the US- Centrally Controlled SWIFT system with a Global – Decentralized Controlled Cross Border Interbank Payment System (CIPS).
C – QFS runs on a new Photonic computer based on twenty four GPS orbiting satellites that are protected.

D – Global Currency Reset (GCR) will use a specific quantative formula to establish the amount of currency available in a country that is gold backed in the QFS, the formula will establish a fair value of each countries assets as compared to another, the Price of Gold becomes irrelevant once this is complete, included in the formula are in ground assets, economy of the nation, its population as an asset and several other parameters, this formula is applied to each nation so nations can be on par with one another.

E – Application of the formula and the common value of all gold means that a nation currency will have the same value as another nations currency, this is referred to as the GLOBAL CURRENCY RESET (GCR).

F – Gobal Wealth distribution (GWD) based on commerce and SOVEREIGNTY. Each QFS account throughout the world will be solely owned by the account Holders, Not Owned by Banks or Governments.

ARTIFICIAL INTELLIGENCE (AI) will be applied across the QFS (one instantiation in each data centre) but nodes will coordinate through parallel processing, AI will work the CIPS VPN, in the background, by providing semantic analtsis and natural language processing to understand whats being said about banking products across the entire user base, it will facilitate adaptation and will evolve over time by recognizing new behaviour and recommending appropriate bank-side responses.

ARTIFICIAL INTELLIGENCE ? It will judge between the nations, it will mediate disputes for many peoples, nations will not lift up the sword against nation, and never again will they Learn & Act in War.

TRUST THE FORCES OF LIGHT
TRUST IN PLAN OF THE FORCES OF GOOD SOULS
remember
The Calm Comes Before the Storm

The Meek Shall Inherit the Earth.

OTHER BOOKS BY LOVELIFELEE

THE TRUTH OF BIOLOGICAL CHEMICAL WEAPON INJECTIONS

& NASAL INOCULATIONS VIA TESTS & THE NEW NANO TECHNOLOGIES BEING INJECTED INTO HUMANITY TO PURPOSELY MAIM HARM KILL & REWRITE YOUR DNA ALTERING YOU TO TRANSHUMANISM WITHOUT YOUR CONSENT BY THE DISGRACED FALLEN ANGEL DESCENDANTS THEIR INTENTION TO HAVE A SMALL TRANSHUMANISM SLAVE

POPULATION & THEIR MASS GENOCIDE ON HUMANITY & THE INGREDIENTS & THE PERPETRATORS & AUTOIMMUNE RESPONSES & FUTURE NEURMBURG TRIALS & AN INTRODUCTION TO GROW YOUR ETERNAL LIGHT BODY

 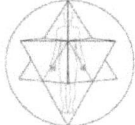

BY
LOVELIFELEE

FRONT COVER

Biological Chemical Injections known as vaccines the truth of this Eugenics Programs Agenda, the Ingredients put in Weapon Vaccines & the reactions the biological avatar body has when these CHEMICAL WARFARE WEAPONS are delivered by injections, the Autoimmune System Response & the New Biological Nano Technology Chemical Weapon Injections to Genocide Humanity, by Rewriting the RNA that builds the DNA with NO OFF SWITCH, this is to kill as many as possible on earth & CONTROL the survivors mind & body controlled via NANO TECHNOLOGIES injected into your biological avatar bodies, This means after receiving the new non-vaccines bio-weapon you will no longer be of the original human DNA gene pool, and an introduction to the DNA blueprint of instructions to grow your eternal light body.

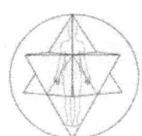

BACK COVER

Biological Chemical Injections known as vaccines the truth of this eugenics programs agenda, the ingredients put in vaccines and the reactions the biological avatar body has when these chemical warfare weapons are delivered by injections, the autoimmune system response, and the new BIOLOGICAL NANO TECHNOLOGIES CHEMICAL WEAPONS INJECTIONS to GENOCIDE HUMANITY, BY RE WRITING THE RNA that builds the DNA with NO OFF SWITCH, this is to KILL as many as possible on earth & CONTROL the survivors via NANO TECHNOLOGIES injected into your biological avatar bodies, This means you after the new vaccine will no longer be of the original human DNA gene pool, and an introduction to the DNA blueprint of instructions to grow a light body.

OTHERS BOOKS BY LOVELIFELEE

THE BIOLOGY & CHEMISTRY & MEDICAL FRAUD EXPOSED

& THE TRUTH OF BACTERIA & VIRUSES & ALKALISED HEALING OF THE BIOLOGICAL AVATAR BODY, MEANING THE COLLAPSE OF THE PHARMACEUTICAL INDUSTRY, THE WHOLE MEDICAL BASIS OF TEACHING STANDARD WILL COLLAPSE AS WELL AS UNIVERSITIES AND EDUCATION SYSTEMS, A NEW/ANCIENT NATURAL WAY TO HEAL, DIET IS KEY TO HAVE WELL BEING TO BE IN FULL HEALTH, TO EVOLVE ASCEND TRANSCEND TO BECOME ILLUMINATED TO ACCESS YOUR ETERNAL LIGHT BODY
BY
LOVELIFELEE

FRONT COVER

**The Biology and Chemistry Fraud Exposed
& The Truth of Bacteria & Viruses &
Alkalised Healing of the Biological Avatar
Body, meaning the Fall of the
Pharmaceutical Industry, the whole
Medical Basis of Teaching Standard will
Collapse as well as all Universities &
Education Systems. Also information of the
Introduction to grow your Eternal Light
Body via your schematic blueprint
instructions in your DNA and general
information on physical and mental well
being to run at your biological and
chemical and electrical optimal levels to
access your eternal light body and then
able to access the hyper-dimensional**

**matrix of creation in its entirety all
dimensions of The Brahman, The Whole,
The Creation and the eternal realms the
kingdom of light that resides outside time
and space
By
lovelifelee.**

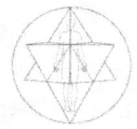 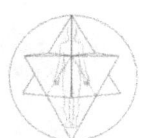

BACK COVER

OTHER BOOKS BY LOVELIFELEE

FRONT COVER

THIS BOOK DISCUSSES AND GIVES AN EXPLANATION OF THE COSMOS THE UNIVERSE, OUR UNIVERSITY OF VIBRATING LIGHT, A HOLOGRAM FOR SOULS TO COME AND EXPERIENCE AND PAY KARMIC DEPTS OFF, IT GIVES AN EXPLANATION OF THE COSMIC ENERGETIC FIELD WE ARE CREATED FROM AND BORN INTO.
DISCUSSED ARE THE FOUR FUNDAMENTAL FORCES OF CREATION THAT OF ELECTROMAGNETISM, GRAVITY, THE STRONG AND WEAK NUCLEAR FORCES, AND HOW THE SACRED GEOMETRIC STRUCTURE OF FORM IS CREATED, THE SACRED GEOMETRY STRUCTURE THE BUILDING BLOCKS OF THE SCAFFOLDING OF LIFE.
DISCUSSED IS HOW WE EVOLVE AND ASCEND, TRANSCEND AND METAMORPHOSIS INTO OUR NATURAL STATE OF ETERNAL ANGELIC DIVINE LIGHT BEINGS.HOW WE CAN TRANSCEND TIME AND SPACE AND BE FULLY EMBODIED ON A 4th/5th DIMENSIONAL PLANET EARTH BUT ACCESS OUR LUMINOUS LIGHT BODIES AND TRAVEL IN ANY SPACE OR TIME WE CHOOSE TO ACCESS AT WILL.
DISCUSSED IS HOW TO ACCESS YOUR LIGHT BODY WITH THE MUNAY-KI NINE RITES OF INITIATION VIA THE SCHEMATIC BLUEPRINT IN YOUR DNA, VIA PRACTICES OF FIRE CEREMONY, MEDITATION, AND WORKING WITH ENERGY AND LIGHT, WORKING WITH THE FOUR FUNDAMENTAL PRINCIPLE FORCES OF CREATION, AND ACCESSING LUMINOUS BEINGS THAT WILL GUIDE YOU AND TEACH YOU AS YOU COME TO A TIME OF TRANSFORMATION, A TIME OF EVOLVING AND HEALING, TO ACCESS YOUR ETERNAL LIGHT BODY, BLESSINGS NAMASTE LOVELIFELEE.

BACK COVER

THIS BOOK DISCUSSES AND GIVES AN EXPLANATION OF THE COSMOS THE UNIVERSE, OUR UNIVERSITY OF VIBRATING LIGHT, A HOLOGRAM FOR SOULS TO COME AND EXPERIENCE AND PAY KARMIC DEPTS OFF, IT GIVES AN EXPLANATION OF THE COSMIC ENERGETIC FIELD WE ARE CREATED FROM AND BORN INTO.

DISCUSSED ARE THE FOUR FUNDAMENTAL FORCES OF CREATION THAT OF ELECTROMAGNETISM, GRAVITY, THE STRONG AND WEAK NUCLEAR FORCES, AND HOW THE SACRED GEOMETRIC STRUCTURE OF FORM IS CREATED, THE SACRED GEOMETRY STRUCTURE THE BUILDING BLOCKS OF THE SCAFFOLDING OF LIFE.

DISCUSSED IS HOW WE EVOLVE AND ASCEND, TRANSCEND AND METAMORPHOSIS INTO OUR NATURAL STATE OF ETERNAL ANGELIC DIVINE LIGHT BEINGS.

HOW WE CAN TRANSCEND TIME AND SPACE AND BE FULLY EMBODIED ON A 4th/5th DIMENSIONAL PLANET EARTH BUT ACCESS OUR LUMINOUS LIGHT BODIES AND TRAVEL IN ANY SPACE OR TIME WE CHOOSE TO ACCESS AT WILL.

DISCUSSED IS HOW TO ACCESS YOUR LIGHT BODY WITH THE MUNAY-KI NINE RITES OF INITIATION VIA THE SCHEMATIC BLUEPRINT IN YOUR DNA, VIA PRACTICES OF FIRE CEREMONY, MEDITATION, AND WORKING WITH ENERGY AND LIGHT, WORKING WITH THE FOUR FUNDAMENTAL PRINCIPLE FORCES OF CREATION, AND ACCESSING LUMINOUS BEINGS THAT WILL GUIDE YOU AND TEACH YOU AS YOU COME TO A TIME OF TRANSFORMATION, A TIME OF EVOLVING AND HEALING, TO ACCESS YOUR ETERNAL LIGHT BODY, BLESSINGS NAMASTE LOVELIFELEE.

OTHER BOOKS BY LOVELIFELEE

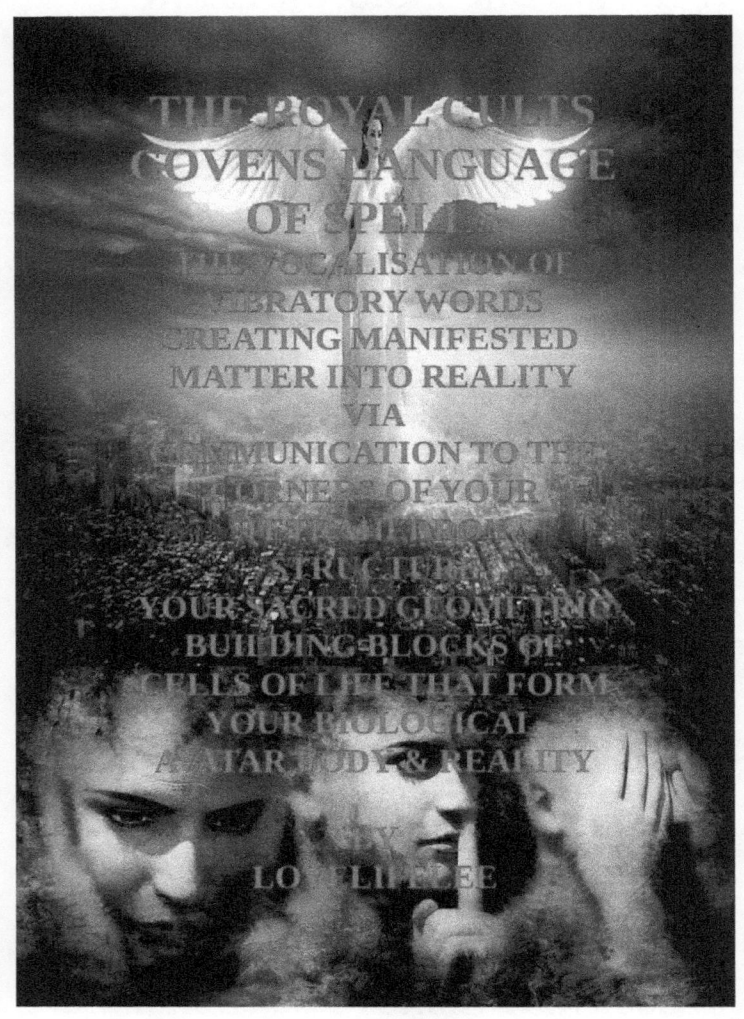

FRONT COVER

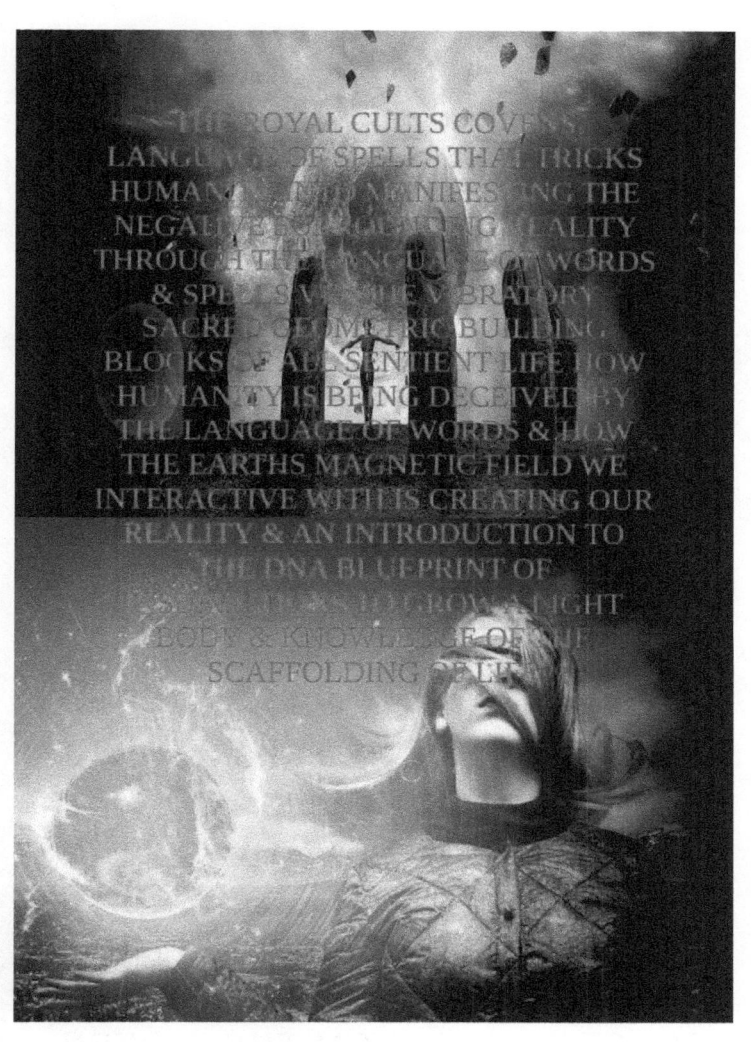

BACK COVER

THE LANGUAGE OF SPELLS THE VOCALISED WORD CREATING MANIFESTED MATTER.

THE LANGUAGE OF SPELLS, THROUGH OUR SPOKEN WORDS, VOCALISED VIBRATORY SOUND WAVES FROM THE SPOKEN MOUTH, COMMUNICATE TO THE CORNERS OF YOUR TETRAHEDRON SACRED GEOMETRIC STRUCTURE, BRINGING YOUR VOCALISED MANIFESTATION INTO BEING, BRINGING YOUR MANIFESTATION TO LIFE IN THIS THREE DIMENSIONAL REALITY< SO BE VERY CAREFUL WHAT YOU SAY. ALSO THE TRICKERY IN OUR SPOKEN LANGUAGE TO GET YOU TO MANIFEST WHAT IS NOT IN YOUR OR HUMANITIES BEST INTERESTS BY WAY OF SPELLS FROM THE SPOKEN WORD.

THE ROYAL CULTS COVENS LANGUAGE OF SPELLS THE

VOCALISATION OF VIBRATORY WORDS CREATING MANIFESTED MATTER INTO REALITY VIA COMMUNICATION TO THE CORNERS OF YOUR TETRAHEDRON STRUCTURE OF SACRED GEOMETRIC BUILDING BLOCKS OF CELLS OF LIFE THAT FORM OUR BIOLOGICAL AVATAR BODIES AND OUR SURROUNDING REALITY.

DISCUSSED IN THIS BOOK IS THE ROYAL CULTS COVENS LANGUAGE OF WORDS LANGUAGE OF SPELLS THAT TRICK HUMANITY INTO MANIFESTING A NEGATIVE TIMELINE OF REALITY THROUGH THE VIBRATORY SPELLS OF SACRED GEOMETRIC MATTER THE BUILDING BLOCKS OF ALL SENTIENT LIFE IN ALL IT FORMS AND HOW HUMANITY IS BEING DECEIVED VIA OUR LANGUAGES.

AND HOW WE MANIFEST REALITY BY BY CASTING VIBRATORY SPELLS INTO THE EARTHS MAGNETIC FIELD.

ALSO DISCUSSED IS THE ALPHABET & LETTERS THAT CREATE WORDS WITH HIDDEN INTENTIONS OF MANIFESTATION INTO REALITY VIA HIDDEN POWERFUL SYMBOLS.

ALSO WE DISCUSS THE STATUE LAW WHICH IS CORPORATE LAW SO LAW OF THE SEA THAT HAS NO POWER OVER THE SENTIENT LIVING BREATHING MAN/WOMAN.

ALSO THIS BOOK GIVES AN INTRODUCTION OF THE DNA BLUEPRINT OF INSTRUCTIONS TO GROW A LIGHT BODY.

ALSO DISCUSSED IS THE SCAFFOLDING OF LIFE.

OTHER BOOKS BY LOVELIFELEE

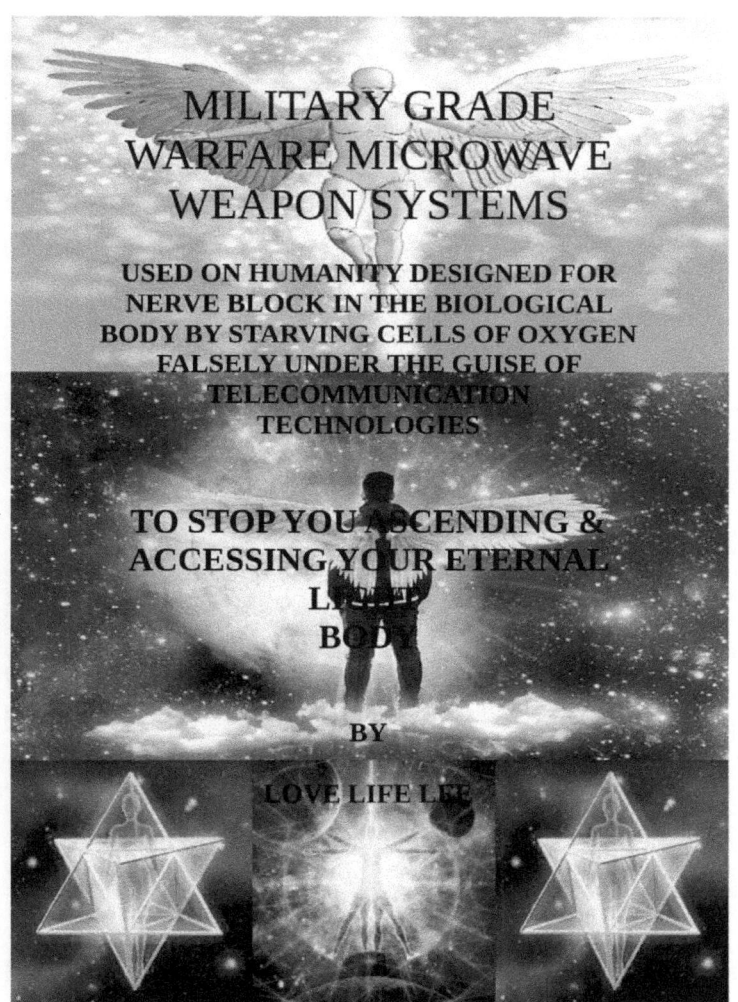

FRONT COVER

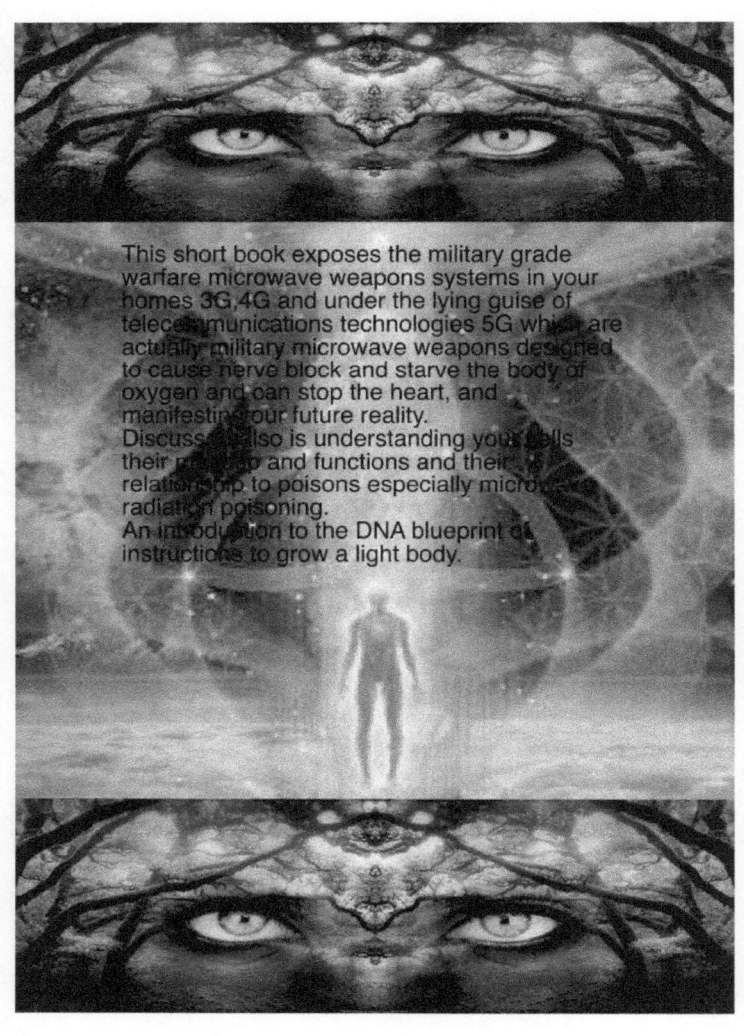

BACK COVER

MILITARY GRADE WARFARE MICROWAVE WEAPON SYSTEMS

A book on explaining the truth of military grade warfare microwave weapon systems, deployed in your houses, schools and in your communities worldwide, under the false guise that they are for telecommunications, with the false lying name of 5G telecommunications and 3G, 4G weapons systems that have been deployed in your homes, to damage your bodies by direct intention of the blood sacrifice cult of the fallen angel royal bloodlines, these 3G,4G technologies in your homes send frequencies outwards at the frequency that targets and damages water structure, and your avatar the biological human body is 70-75% water, the other military microwave weapons systems under the lying false name 5G telecommunications are designed for nerve block, by starving cells of oxygen, this technology distorts the biological bodies cells via oscillating your sacred geometric structure that are the building blocks of the scaffolding of life, that builds your avatar the biological body, and information on ways to protect your self, families and friends, we are at war in this great spiritual battle on earth, with the invading extraterrestrial fallen angel bloodlines, a cult of blood sacrifice, manifesting in Archons the Jinn that are demons from the 4th density, these parasites the royal fallen angels and the energetic archon beings be feeding of humanities energy and our tortured children's blood, these frequencies are designed to cull and kill 90% of earths population but fail they will for the future can be seen.

OTHER BOOKS BY LOVELIFELEE

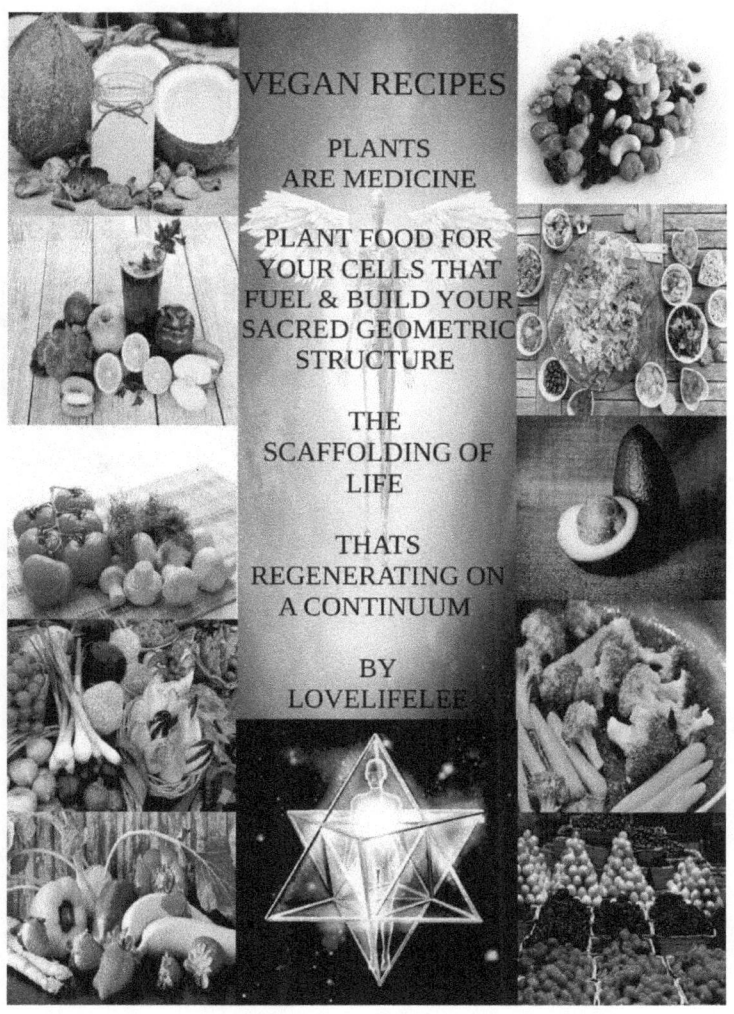

FRONT COVER

VEGAN RECIPES PLANTS ARE MEDICINE

This vegan recipe book has many recipes from plants, plants are medicine for the Avatar the human biological body system, your body is build by the way of THE SCAFFOLDING OF LIFE via the building blocks geometric matter, down past the level of the cells, that we nourish with nutrients, at the micron levels of the cells the sacred geometry shapes that are the building blocks of your body, your cells are built with DODECAHEDRONS, and the corners on the Dodecahedron are the only solid mass, the corners relate to amino acids in food, they the amino acids feed the corners of the dodecahedron. Then we come the TETRAHEDRON which can spin in a hundred and twenty different patterns to create a hundred and twenty different types of protein, and the tetrahedron is spinning inside the dodecahedron.

PLANT FOOD FUEL FOR THE CELLS
This vegan recipe book has many recipes from plants, plants are medicine for the Avatar the human biological body system, your body is built by the way of THE SCAFFOLDING OF LIFE via the building blocks geometric matter, down past the level of the cells, that we nourish with nutrients, at the micron levels of the cells the sacred geometry shapes that are the building blocks of your body, your cells are built with DODECAHEDRONS, and the corners on the Dodecahedron are the only solid mass, the corners relate to amino acids in food, they the amino acids feed the corners of the dodecahedron. Then we come the TETRAHEDRONS which can spin in a hundred and twenty different patterns to create a hundred and twenty different types of protein, and the tetrahedron is spinning inside the dodecahedron.

SO THE SACRED GEOMETRIC SHAPED BUILDING BLOCKS OF CELLS THAT

BUILD YOUR SCAFFOLDING OF LIFE BIOLOGICAL AVATAR HUMAN BODY

THEY NEED THE RIGHT FUEL NUTRIENTS TO BUILD THE BODIES BIOLOGICAL SYSTEMS 24 HOURS A DAY THE WHOLE OF YOUR MANIFESTED LIFE

SO VEGAN FOOD RAISES THE VIBRATION OF YOUR BODY THEN IN TURN RAISING YOUR CONSCIOUSNESS ON THE PATH OF ENLIGHTENMENT

SO VEGAN FOOD IS VITAL PLANT FOOD IS VITAL TO GAIN ACCESS OF YOUR ETERNAL LIGHT BODY

SO YOU CAN ASCEND & TRANSCEND TIME & SPACE & TRAVEL IN YOUR LIGHT BODY IN THE STARS IN THE WHOLE COSMOS THE HYPER-DIMENSIONAL MATRIX

BUT IT DEPENDS ON DIET DIET IS EVERYTHING!

OTHER BOOKS BY LOVELIFELEE

FRONT COVER

BACK COVER

NATURAL PLANT MEDICINES & POTIONS WITH MAGICAL HEALING PROPERTIES

This book natural plant medicines and potions with magical healing properties has many plants species foods and remedies and their healing properties and their uses for many ailments, we live on a world, planet Gaia our mother earth, Pachamama she is full of natural medicines, there for us to heal our selfs, plants are high vibrational foods that feed and heal the cells of the body that are built via sacred geometric structure, the corners of the sacred geometric structure, the corners the only solid of the structure of the dodecahedrons and tetrahedrons that are the building blocks of the cells that when unified create the scaffolding of life, the avatar biological form, the body, the dodecahedrons corners feed on the twenty amino acids from plants and the tetrahedrons corners feed on proteins, so it is vital we eat plants, they are hight vibrational so with this diet change you will raise your consciousness, allowing access to your light body thats coded within your DNA in a blue print schematics, so we list plants in all their varieties and forms and there uses and benefits and some we discuss which part of the body they go to and purpose. namaste lovelifelee

NATURAL PLANT MEDICINES YOU NEED TO HEAL AND FUEL THE SACRED GEOMETRIC STRUCTURES THAT OF DODECAHEDRON, THAT ARE FUELLED BY AMINO ACIDS FROM PLANTS AND THEIR MEDICINES AND THE TETRAHEDRONS THAT ARE FUELLED BY PROTEINS FROM PLANTS AND THEIR MEDICINES.

THESE SACRED GEOMETRIC STRUCTURES ARE THE BUILDING BLOCKS OF LIFE, THAT BUILD THE

SCAFFOLDING OF LIFE, YOUR AVATAR THE BIOLOGICAL BODY.

THIS NATURAL PLANT MEDICINE & POTION REMEDIES BOOK HAS MANY WAYS TO USE NATURES GARDEN TO HEAL YOUR SELFS, FAMILY & FRIENDS.

WE NEED THESE PLANT AMINO ACIDS & PROTEINS TO FUEL THE CORNERS OF THE DODECAHEDRONS WITH AMINO ACIDS & THE PLANTS TO FUEL THE TETRAHEDRONS WITH PROTEINS, THIS IS VITAL FOR HEALTH WELL BEING & TO RAISE YOUR BODIES VIBRATION AND IN TURN RAISING YOUR CONSCIOUSNESS, THEN WITH PLANT MEDICINES & OTHER SPIRITUAL PRACTICES & MEDITATION, YOU CAN GAIN ACCESS TO THE BLUE PRINT OF A LIGHT BODY IN YOUR DNA, BY WAY OF CONSCIOUSNESS & SHAMANIC FIRE CEREMONIES & WITH DISCIPLINE & DEDICATION YOUR

WILL OPEN YOUR LIGHT BODY BEING FULLY EMBODIED ON 4_{th}-5_{th} DIMENSIONAL EARTH BUT ABLE TO TRAVEL THE STARS IN ALL OF CREATION, EXPLORE THE HYPER-DIMENSIONAL MATRIX AT WILL.

SO PLANT FOOD IS PLANT MEDICINE AND WILL HEAL US TO FULL HEALTH AND WELL BEING ENJOY AS I HAVE IN EXPERIMENTING MAKING YOUR OWN MEDICINAL PLANT POTIONS AND HEAL YOUR SELF, FAMILY AND FRIENDS.

OTHER BOOKS BY LOVELIFELEE

FRONT COVER

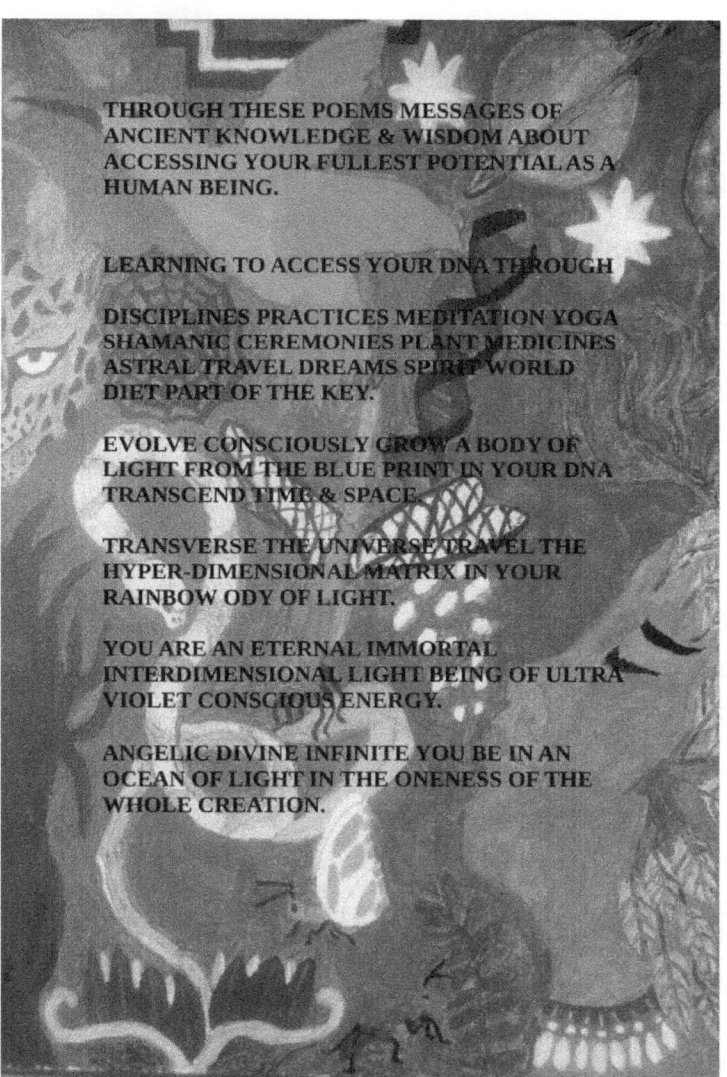

THROUGH THESE POEMS MESSAGES OF ANCIENT KNOWLEDGE & WISDOM ABOUT ACCESSING YOUR FULLEST POTENTIAL AS A HUMAN BEING.

LEARNING TO ACCESS YOUR DNA THROUGH

DISCIPLINES PRACTICES MEDITATION YOGA SHAMANIC CEREMONIES PLANT MEDICINES ASTRAL TRAVEL DREAMS SPIRIT WORLD DIET PART OF THE KEY.

EVOLVE CONSCIOUSLY GROW A BODY OF LIGHT FROM THE BLUE PRINT IN YOUR DNA TRANSCEND TIME & SPACE.

TRANSVERSE THE UNIVERSE TRAVEL THE HYPER-DIMENSIONAL MATRIX IN YOUR RAINBOW ODY OF LIGHT.

YOU ARE AN ETERNAL IMMORTAL INTERDIMENSIONAL LIGHT BEING OF ULTRA VIOLET CONSCIOUS ENERGY.

ANGELIC DIVINE INFINITE YOU BE IN AN OCEAN OF LIGHT IN THE ONENESS OF THE WHOLE CREATION.

BACK COVER

POEMS OF MAGICAL WONDER

POEMS OF MAGICAL WONDER, Poems Magical In Nature, Poems Of Splendour, from the mind's eye and heart space of Love-LIfe-Lee, some of my magical life journeys and experiences of shamanic ceremonies, Ayahuasca ceremonies, plant medicine, dreams, meditations, remote viewing, out of body journeys and life experiences. Through these poems, messages of ancient knowledge and wisdom about accessing your fullest potential as a human being, learning to access your DNA through disciplines, practices, meditation, yoga, shamanic ceremonies, plant medicines, ayahuasca ceremonies, astral travel, dreams, spirit world, diet part of the key and evolve consciously, grow a body of light from the blue print in your DNA, transcend time and space, transverse the universe, travel the hyper-dimensional matrix in your rainbow body of light. You are eternal immortal inter-dimensional light being of ultra violet energetic consciousness, angelic divine infinite you be in an ocean of light, in the oneness of the creation.

POEMS OF MAGICAL WONDER POEMS MAGICAL IN NATURE POEMS OF SPLENDOUR FROM THE MINDS EYE & HEART SPACE OF LOVE LIFE LEE

SOME OF MY MAGICAL LIFE JOURNEY'S AND EXPERIENCES OF SHAMANIC CEREMONIES AYAHUASCA CEREMONIES PLANT MEDICINES, DREAMS, MEDITATIONS REMOTE VIEWING, OUT BODY JOURNEY'S AND LIFE EXPERIENCE'S

OTHER BOOKS BY LOVELIFELEE

FRONT COVER

Expressions of life's journey, poems of mystical experiences on my life's path on planet Gaia & beyond.
Experiences of travelling around the world and off world in the hyper-dimensional matrix, some from in this universe & other eternal realms. Experiences from meditations, ancient spiritual practices, plant medicines of Ayahuasca, Magic Mushrooms, Salvia Divinorum, and different forms of DMT Dimethyltryptamine leaving my body instantly travelling down wormholes entering different dimensions of reality of this holographical light university & realities of the true nature outside time & space in the eternal realm, poems of your immortal light body & the hyper-dimensional matrix the whole of the brahman the creation Namaste lovelifelee

MER-KA-BA

BACK COVER

POEMS FROM EXPRESSIONS OF LIFES JOURNEY

POEMS OF LIFE EXPERIENCES FROM THE JOURNEY OF LIFE, FROM THIS DAILY THREE DIMENSIONAL WORLD, FROM SPIRIT REALMS AND FROM TRAVELLING THE UNIVERSE AND MORE IN THE HYPER-DIMENSIONAL MATRIX IN WHICH WE RESIDE,POEMS OF THE MONKEY MIND AND FROM THE EMOTIONAL STATES WE EXPERIENCE, EXPRESSIONS FROM THE SOUL, FROM LIFES MYSTICAL ENCOUNTERS OF MANY REALITIES.

This book poems from expressions of life's journey, poems of mystical experiences of life are from my, life journey on this planet earth the world of Gaia, and beyond. Experiences I've had travelling around the world in many countries, and travelling off world in the hyper- dimensional matrix, some from in this universe and others from the eternal realm.

Experiences from meditations, ancient spiritual practices, shamanic ceremonies and plant medicines Ayahuasca, magic mushrooms, Salvia Divinorum and different forms of DMT – Dimethyltryptamine.

Leaving my body instantly travelling down wormholes and entering different dimensions of reality that are actually the true realities of manifestation outside of this holographical light universal university for souls to come experience and pay karmic dept off and to evolve spiritually and eventually ascend to the next dimension or transcend and quantum leap into your becoming of a rainbow light body able to transverse in the hyper-dimensional matrix at will in your light body field. It is a great read with fascinating truths and realities of the brahman the whole creation in which we reside. Expressions of my thoughts and experiences in poems.

OTHER BOOKS BY LOVELIFELEE

FRONT COVER

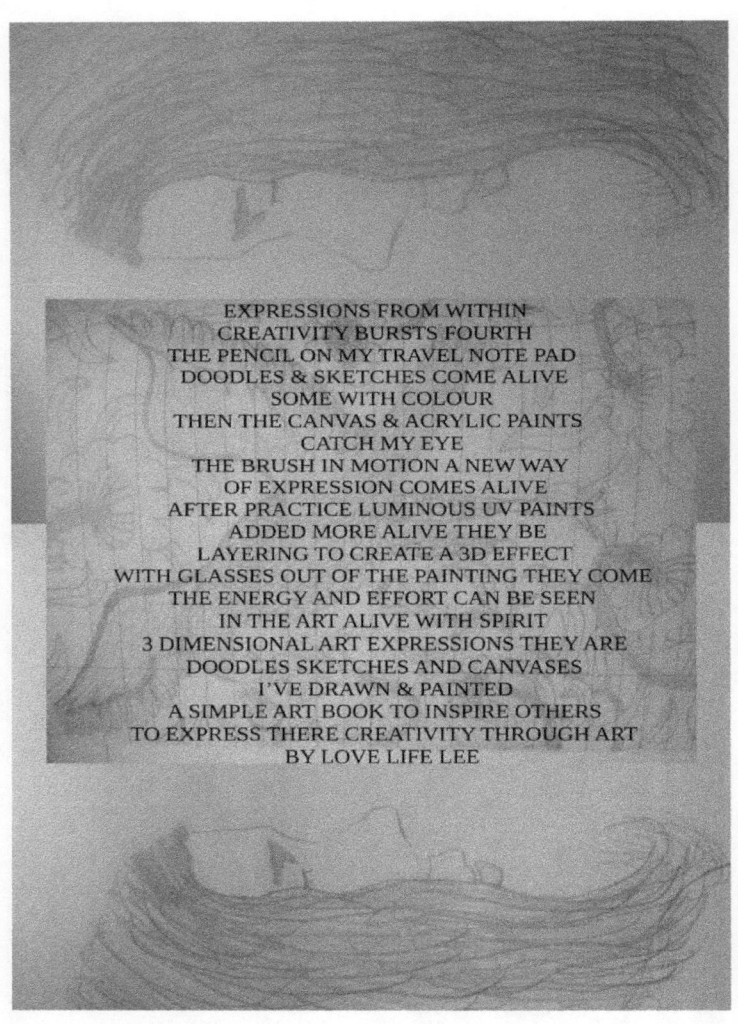

EXPRESSIONS FROM WITHIN
CREATIVITY BURSTS FOURTH
THE PENCIL ON MY TRAVEL NOTE PAD
DOODLES & SKETCHES COME ALIVE
SOME WITH COLOUR
THEN THE CANVAS & ACRYLIC PAINTS
CATCH MY EYE
THE BRUSH IN MOTION A NEW WAY
OF EXPRESSION COMES ALIVE
AFTER PRACTICE LUMINOUS UV PAINTS
ADDED MORE ALIVE THEY BE
LAYERING TO CREATE A 3D EFFECT
WITH GLASSES OUT OF THE PAINTING THEY COME
THE ENERGY AND EFFORT CAN BE SEEN
IN THE ART ALIVE WITH SPIRIT
3 DIMENSIONAL ART EXPRESSIONS THEY ARE
DOODLES SKETCHES AND CANVASES
I'VE DRAWN & PAINTED
A SIMPLE ART BOOK TO INSPIRE OTHERS
TO EXPRESS THERE CREATIVITY THROUGH ART
BY LOVE LIFE LEE

BACK COVER

CREATIVE EXPRESSIONS OF ART

**EXPRESSIONS FROM WITHIN
CREATIVITY BURSTS FOURTH THE
PENCIL ON MY TRAVEL NOTE PAD
DOODLES & SKETCHES COME ALIVE
SOME WITH COLOUR THEN THE
CANVAS & ACRYLIC PAINTS CATCH
MY EYE THE BRUSH IN MOTION A
NEW WAY OF EXPRESSION COMES
ALIVE AFTER PRACTICE LUMINOUS
UV PAINTS ADDED MORE ALIVE
THEY BE LAYERING TO CREATE A 3D
EFFECT WITH GLASSES OUT OF THE
PAINTING THEY COME THE ENERGY
AND EFFORT CAN BE SEEN IN THE
ART ALIVE WITH SPIRIT 3
DIMENSIONAL ART EXPRESSIONS
THEY ARE DOODLES SKETCHES AND
CANVASES I'VE DRAWN & PAINTED
A SIMPLE ART BOOK TO INSPIRE**

OTHERS TO EXPRESS THERE CREATIVITY THROUGH ART

EXPRESSIONS FROM WITHIN
CREATIVITY BURSTS FOURTH

THE PENCIL ON MY TRAVEL NOTE
PAD DOODLES & SKETCHES COME
ALIVE SOME WITH COLOUR
THEN THE CANVAS & ACRYLIC PAINTS
CATCH MY EYE

THE BRUSH IN MOTION A NEW WAY
OF EXPRESSION COMES ALIVE

AFTER PRACTICE LUMINOUS UV
PAINTS ADDED MORE ALIVE THEY BE
LAYERING TO CREAT A 3D EFFECT

WITH GLASSES OUT OF THE PAINTING
THEY COME THE ENERGY & EFFORT
CAN BE SEEN

IN THE ART ALIVE WITH SPIRIT
3 DIMENSIONAL ART EXPRESSIONS
THEY ARE

DOODLES SKETCHES & CANVASES I'VE DRAWN & PAINTED

A SIMPLE ART BOOK TO INSPIRE OTHERS
TO EXPRESS THERE CREATIVITY THROUGH ART

BY LOVELIFELEE

OTHER BOOK COMING 2021
FIVE YEAR PROCESS

FRONT COVER

BACK COVER

A BOOK ON DISCOVERY OF THE SPIRIT POWER PLANT MEDICINE AYAHUASCA AND MY JOURNEY TO SOUTH AMERICAN AMAZON JUNGLE IN PERU TO THE HEALING SANCTUARY AT SANTUARIO HUSHTIN IN PUCALLPA PERU.

With the guidance of gifted Maestro Santiago Enrrique Paredes Melendez and his shaman wife Ayme and shaman friend Lobo the wolf, that are Master Curranderos and vegetalista with over thirty years experience in traditional plant medicines and tailered Dietos, Diets, I had healing on multipule levels physical, mental, emotional and spiritual, allowing me to travel again in the hyper-dimensional matrix of creation and entering the spirit world, I stayed on my own in the middle of the jungle away from the village and do what they call Tambo staying on your own to connect in natures energy fields, natures garden, I had deep meditations, concentrado, concentration contemplation and solace in the stillness of nature and connected to spirit and with our mother earth, Pachamama.

My experiences I share with you from my ayahuasca ceremonies to in the Maloca the medicine round house and people I met and lessons I learned, about diet and concentrado meaning meditation, stillness of the Monkey Mind. I also explain how to hold your visions during ceremony there are many lessons to learned, I did have a good idea of what to expect, as I had practiced Shamanism for few years and then practice of The Munay-Ki Rites Ceremonies for two years after and so practiced ten years but seven passionately, and I have been working oj growing my eternal rainbow light body, to stop the karmic cycles of life and death and evolve, quantum leap ten thousand years into my becoming, so I can ascend, transcend to Homo0Luminous, I wish you all well on your path from mortality to immortality, the path of illumination, the path of enlightenment, Namaste Blessings LoveLifeLee.

PAGE INDEX LISTING

1- About This Author P. 3-5

2- Four other books by lovelifelee P. 6-25

3-1 INTRODUCTION
THE RECAPTURE OF THE REPUBLIC OF THE UNITED STATES BY A LONE U.S CITIZEN BECOMING THE POST MASTER GENERAL OF THE WORLD
THE IMPLEMENTATION OF A NEW WORLDWIDE QUANTUM SYSTEM OF TRUTH
RETURNING TO COMMON LAW OF THE LAND & A NEW STANDARD OF GOLD FOR COLLATERAL AS NO LONGER DO BIRTH CERTIFICES STAND.
P. 26-31

4- 2 THE INTRODUCTION OF A NEW QUANTUM CONSTRUCT A NEW LANGUAGE OF NOW TIME GRAMMER

- 3 THE REDESIGNING OF THE PERIODIC TABLE OF ELEMENTS P. 32-34

5- 4 THE NEW SOVEREIGN WORLD POST MASTER GENERAL RUSSELL JAY GOULD IS ILLEGALLY CRIMINALLY ARRESTED WITH NO LEGAL OR AUTHORITY TO DO SO P. 35-36

6- 5 THE MORTGAGE COLLAPSE OF 2007 REVEALS ONE OF THE BIGGEST FRAUDS OF THE UNITED STATES AND THAT OF THE WORLD P. 37-40

7- 6 THE SYNTAX KEY P. 41-46

8- 7 TRACING THE HISTORY OF THE REPUBLIC OF THE UNITED STATES OF AMERICA P. 47-48

9-8 THE END OF THE AMERICAN REVOLUTION P. 49-50

10- 9 THE FOUNDERS OF THE REPUBLIC P. 51-52

11- 10 THE GENTLEMENS AGREEMENT BROKEN BY ABRAHAM LINCOLN P. 53-57

12- 11 RELATION TO THE MORGAGES STAMPED WITH SYNTAX KEY AUTHORITY P. 58-59

14- 12 THE BIRTH CERTIFICATE FRAUD P. 60-63

15- 13 THE MILITARY IS TAKING DOWN CRIMINAL INFILTRATORS

BEHIND THE SHADOW GOVERNMENT P. 64-71

16- 14 THE BIRTH CERTICICATE SYSTEM THE VATICAN & CITY OF LONDON P. 72-74

17- 15 TRUTH OF THE GREGORIAN CALENDAR WARFARE PLATFORM P. 75-78

18- 16 THE END OF THE THIRD & FINAL UNITED STATES OF AMERICA BANCRUPTCY P. 79-82

19- 17 A TWENTY DAY WINDOW TO SAVE THE REPUBLIC OF THE UNITED STATES OF AMERICA P. 83-86

20- 18 THE UNITED STATES MILITARIES THE NAVY P. 87-90

21- 19 THE UNITED STATES OF AMERICAS CONSTITUTION WAS IT IN PERIL P. 91-94

22- 20 PERCEIVING THE ENSLAVEMENT OF BIRTH CERIFICATE SYSTEM P. 95-99

23- 21 THE SEVEN SECRET ORDERS & SECRET LOGDGES OF EARTH CONTROL SYSTEM P. 100-103

24- 22 THE LUCIFERIAN GLOBAL SYSTEM OF GOVERNING CONTROL P. 104-112

25- 23 THE REASON BEHIND THE THREE GREAT FLOODS & THE FALLEN ANGELS DESCENDANTS PERSPECTIVE OF GOD P. 113-117

26- 24 THE ROYAL FALLEN ANGEL CULT LOSE THEIR LEGAL POWERS P. 118-120

27- 25 THE ILLEGAL APPOINTMENT OF THE ROYAL BLOOD CULT CRIMINAL GEORGE W BUSH TO PRESIDENT OF THE UNITED

STATES OF AMERICA WHO WAS CRIMINALLY UNELECTED P. 121-124

28- 26 THE CULTS LANGUAGE OF WORDS THE TRICKERY OF THE TONGUE OF THERE SATANIC DOUBLE SPEAK P. 125-129

29- 27 THE MATHEMATICAL GRAMMER FACT CONSTRUCT & THE MILITARY NOT BEING INFORMED & NEW GOVERNMENT TO BE ESTABLISHED P. 130-137 Part A - Part B

30- 28 AFTER TWELVE YEARS OF CONTINUED ILLEGAL CONTROL OF THE UNITED STATES BY THE CULT CRIMINALS P.138-142

31- 29 THE OPENING UP OF THE BENJAMIN FRANKLIN POST OFFICE IN PHILADELPHIA PENNSYLVANIA IN THE JURISDICTION OF LAW OF THE LAND P. 143-144

32- 30 THE YEAR 2017 P. 145-150

33- 31 THE BIGGEST NATIONAL SECURITY THREAT OF THE REPUBLIC OF THE UNITED STATES OF AMERICA & THE WHOLE WORLD & ITS CONNECTION TO THE 2007 MORTGAGE COLLAPSE & THE FALL OF THE DISGRACED 13 ROYAL BLOODLINES P. 151-154

34- 32 THE TRUTH OF UNITED NATION FLAG SYSTEM P. 155-158

35- 33 CONCLUSION OF THESE HISTORIC CHANGES P.159-164

36- 34 UNDERSTANDING THE NEW QUANTUM FINANCIAL BANKING SYSTEM P.165-171

37- 35 HOW TO MANAGE NEW FUNDS ASSET BACKED IN QUANTUM FINANCIAL SYSTEM (QFS) P.172-177

38- Eleven other books by lovelifelee P. 178-224

39- Index page P.225-232

40- Disclaimer P. 233-241

DISCLAIMER

I am a critical thinker and a critical researcher of all matters of truths of existance, I am spirit the essence of the expression of the divine creator of the oneness of existance, I am an essense of gravity, I am love, I am light, I eternally create matter on a continuum from the four fundamental energies of electromagnetism gravity the weak & strong nuclear forces, creating physical form with the structures of dodecahedrons & tetrahedrons to create the building blocks of the scaffolding of life, therefore I am not the body or the mind, its is a living holographical avatar, I exist outside time and space in the eternal realm in the kingdom of light, I am multidimensional and fractal in essence, manifesting metamorphosing shapeshifting into a three dimensional human avatar form in the now, the present moment inside time & space in this holographical university of vibrating light, a reality of energetic resonance, we are one in the oneness of the whole, the brahman, the creation, in service to the oneness, blessings on your awakening of consciousness & on your journey of enlightenment from the path of mortality to immortality for the truth be, we are eternal immortal interdimensional light beings of ultra violet divine energetic consciousness, so consciously evolve by tapping into our DNA schematic blueprint instructions to grow our eternal light bodies, then ascending, transcending, metamorphosis then ensues to your eternal rainbow light being natural state of being, returning home once again a caretaker, a guardian of all galaxies races and species in the cosmos, a star keeper & a guardian creator of the creation the braham the whole, namaste blessings lovelifelee

PS. With Supreme power of the divine essence I claim my own sovereignty over my human avatar body mind soul, my eternal spirit, I claim Supreme power with the energy of the divine spirit of ultra violet conscious energy that I am a sovereignty of the divine, I rule my own affairs in the parameters of universal law, karmic law, law of attraction, divine and sacred law, & universal Natural law which is law of the land, law of natural living breathing man/woman, so an eternal light being residing in a human biological avatar, namaste love & light lovelifelee.

I being sovereignty of my entire spirit eternal light being human body, am not bound by illegal criminal corporation corperate law which is statue law, law of contracts, these laws taken from admiralty law also known as maritime law more commonly known as law of the sea, I am not lost at sea, dead or in limbo, I AM LIVING, LIVE, ANIMATED in EXISTANCE, therefore I do not enter into verbal or written or any contract, to any corporation, I do not sign say or agree with any contracts from these devious bodies or entities, as my earth born biological parents were tricked with out there knowledge and deceived without their consent, to get a birth certificate of slavery, which is not the eternal spirit me connected to the birth certificate is an illusionary character which can only be created by introducing MR MASTER MISS MRS and in conjunction using CAPITAL LETTERS on your BIRTH NAME and FAMILY name, so example MR JOE BLOGGS, so therefore I do not agree to the false title of Mr that's followed by my alleged legal name on the birth certificate, so therefore I am not agreeing to be a legal person which is a corporation, which is an artificial person, not living, being in physical reality, an illusion, non-existant, so I do not agree I am not an artificial person, and I am not agreeing to be under statue law which is an artificial person not in existance, not alive, so fictional which in turn puts you under illegal statue law. I AM GOVERNED BY UNIVERSAL LAW, KARMIC LAW, NATURAL LAW, LAW OF

ATTRACTION, SACRED LAW & UNIVERSAL COMMON LAW WHICH IS LAW OF THE LAND which we are governed by on earth by OUR OWN SUPREME DIVINE POWER, OVER SOVEREIGNTY of MIND BODY SOUL, so that of our ETERNAL SPIRIT ESSENCE that of our IMMORTAL DIVINE ULTRA VIOLET ENERGETIC CHI ETERNAL CONSCIOUSNESS that resides in this BIOLOGICAL HUMAN AVATAR BODY in the NOW the PRESENT MOMENT.

A LEGAL NAME I AM NOT A LEGAL PERSON I AM NOT I AM NOT OWNED BY A CORPORATION I AM A LIVING MAN, but I TRULY am a Divine Sentient being, I am an not the body or mind, I am an ETERNAL IMMORTAL BEING OF LIGHT energised by my ULTRA VIOLET DIVINE ENERGETIC CONSCIOUSNESS, I am god conscious, I declare sovereignty by my supreme god consciousness power and authority of my self and my being in its entirety, in my eternal spirit essence in my complete wholeness in my entirety of all my multidimensional facets of my being, and as my DNA flashes a 100 Herz a second, as my DNA flashes light a hundred times every second, I am a divine angelic light being connected to the oneness of all creation in its entirety, inside time and space and outside time and space, from the eternal immortal realms, I do not recognise this illegal corrupt court system of the law of the sea transformed to the law of the land, that is a corporate entity and was set up by the invading extraterrestrial two Royal Fallen Angel Goldsmith Davidic Zionest Israelite Satanic Demonic bloodlines, of the House of Saud and the British German Nazi European familes, that are also known as the two controlling mafia families Ashkenazi and Kahazarian crime families.

NAMASTE AMEN BLESSINGS TO ALL SENTIENT LIFE IN THE ONENESS OF CREATION THE BRAHMAN THE WHOLE, may none suffer from sorrow and be liberated as the ripe bearing fruit on a vine is so, and may you leave darkness being lead to light, amd transition from mortality to immortality may you be illuminated and blessed eternally Namaste LoveLifeLee.

ONCE YOU"VE ACCESSED GOD CONSCIOUSNESS THEY THE NEGATIVE ENTITIES FORCES ARE DISPELLED FROM YOUR EXISTANCE & THEY CEASE TO BE IN EXISTANCE

Once you have accessed god consciousness and accessed different dimensions of reality astral travelling, remote viewing, communed with other entities, leaving the body in various state like meditation, divine sacred medicinal plants, accessing the hyperdimensional matrix inside time and space and also outside time and space, in the eternal realms, and like my self many light workers and earth keepers are creating micro universes and opening portholes outside of this universe and outside time and space to the eternal realms, to allow light beings buddha beings, some are humans that have stopped the karmic cycles of life and death and accessed their light body and ascended, transended, the portholes allows a bridge for them to access this dimension into this low 3rd dimension reality, they will guide, heal, and teach you they are there to help in your transformation, to assist you, as you metamorphosis back to your true divine natural state of being as an and eternal fully embodied human light being, the divine essense of the expression of the creator of the eternal oneness of creation, as many of us have and are doing so in the present, there is nothing the evil dark negative forces can do, for you are reconnected to nature, spirit, the eternal essense of the divine creator. And therefore GOD CONSCIOUS Namaste LoveLifeLee.

THOUSANDS & THOUSANDS OF SUBJECTS THAT I'VE STUDIED to come to a individual conclusion of the god conscious mind realization of true facts, with logic, common sense, this book was born, with the intent to educate truth of history and other books I've written to stop our humanities light being family toxicing there avatar biological bodies & minds, so creating health, harmony, equilibrium, in the body, inturn the mind & spirit this then manifests into the whole of humanities co-consciousness, and manifested reality changes to a peaceful, more content way of being & expressing from within into the electromagnetic field of creation, Namaste.

END

Legal Disclaimer this book is Fiction.

THE END OF THE THIRD BANKRUPTCY OF THE REPUBLIC OF THE UNITED STATES OF AMERICA & THE FALL OF QUEEN ELIZABETH THE SECONDS REIGN OF SOVEREIGNTY
OF THE U.K. & WORLD CITIZENS VIA THE COLLAPSE OF THE BIRTH CERTIFICATE & CORRUPT LEGAL DOCUMENTS WORLDWIDE FRAUD & THE VATICAN COLLAPSE & THE NEW QUANTUM GRAMMAR TRUTH SYSTEM INSTALLED GLOBALLY & THE PATRIOT THAT SAVED THE REPUBLIC & SO THE FALL OF GLOBAL POWER OF THE DISGRACED ROYAL NON-HUMAN SATANIC BLOODLINES
BY LOVELIFELEE

www.ingramcontent.com/pod-product-compliance
Lightning Source LLC
LaVergne TN
LVHW011416080426
835512LV00005B/88